SCOTTISH TREASURES

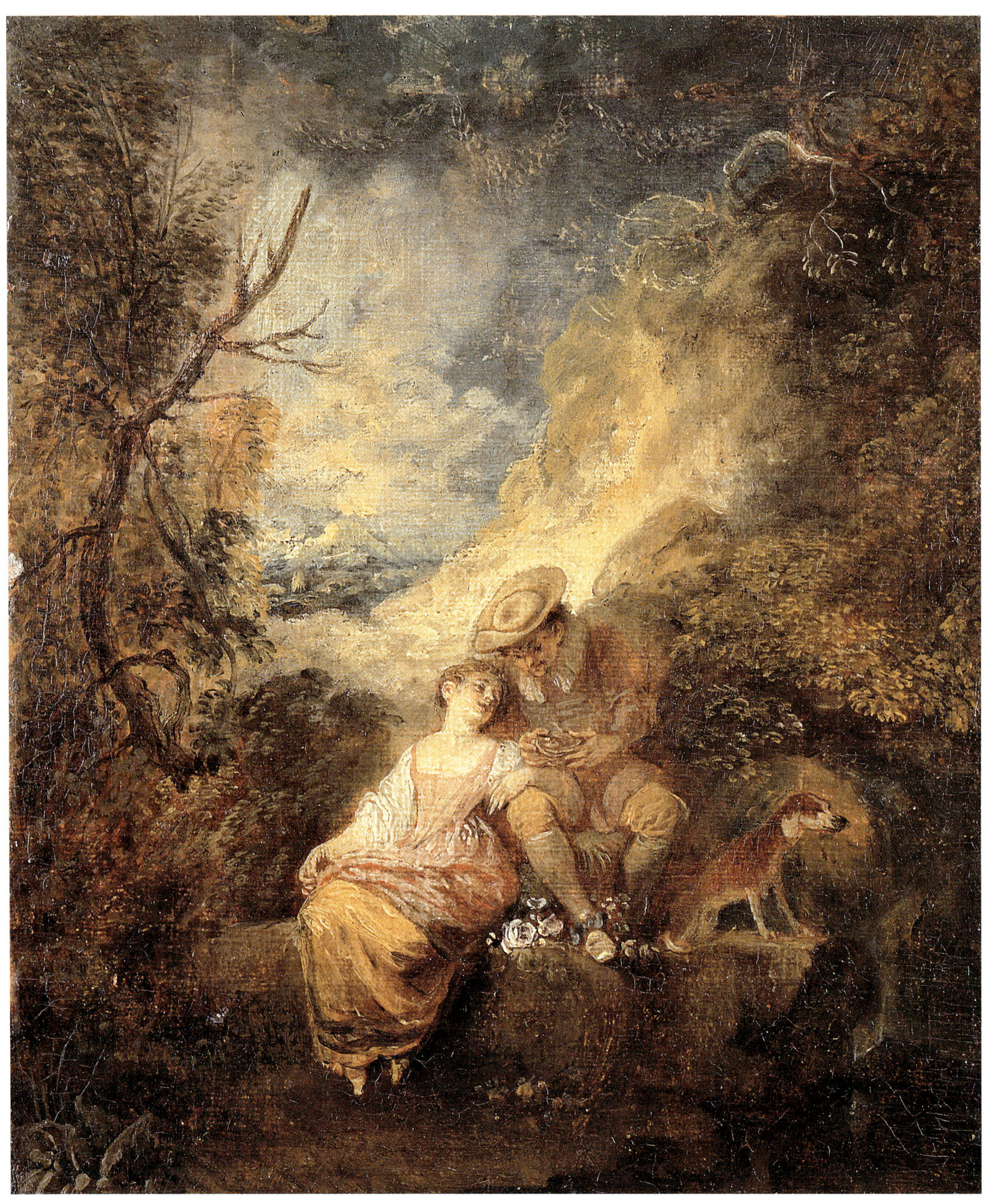

SCOTTISH TREASURES

Masterpieces from the National Gallery of Scotland

NATIONAL GALLERIES
OF SCOTLAND
2001

Published by the Trustees of the National Galleries of Scotland on the occasion of the exhibition *Scottish Treasures: Masterpieces from the National Gallery of Scotland* shown at the Memphis Brooks Museum of Art from March 4 to May 20, 2001, the Georgia Museum of Art from June 9 to September 9, 2001 and the New Orleans Museum of Art from September 22 to December 9, 2001. The American tour has been organised by ArtReach International.

ISBN 1 903278 15 5

Designed and typeset in Hoefler Requiem by Dalrymple
Printed in Belgium by Snoeck-Ducaju & Zoon, Ghent

Cover illustration: detail from Sir Henry Raeburn
Colonel Alastair Ranaldson Macdonell of Glengarry, no. 37

Frontispiece: Jean-Antoine Watteau
The Robber of the Sparrow's Nest, no.25
reproduced at actual size

Contents

Preface

It is a great privilege for us to exhibit some of our wonderful collection to American audiences. We are frequent lenders to the United States, but this is usually in the context of individual loans to specific exhibitions. *Scottish Treasures* enables us to give some indication of the range of masterpieces under our care. We have included paintings which have been acquired at various stages in the National Gallery of Scotland's long history, but we have also deliberately chosen some of our more recent acquisitions. This reflects our belief that collections need to grow if they are to thrive and to continue to stimulate interest and support.

The catalogue of the exhibition has been prepared under the editorship of Michael Clarke (French entries), with contributions from the curatorial staff at the National Gallery, Julia Lloyd Williams (Dutch and Flemish), Helen Smailes (British) and Aidan Weston-Lewis (Italian and Spanish). It has been efficiently seen to press by Janis Adams and Christine Thompson of our Publications Department, and designed by Robert Dalrymple. Our Registrar's Department, headed by Anne Buddle, has supervised all transport arrangements, and the Conservation Department has kindly prepared the loans. The negotiations and arrangements for this exhibition tour have been undertaken by Michael Clarke, Director of the National Gallery of Scotland

We are delighted that the exhibition tour is taking place under the auspices of ArtReach International whose Director, David Setford, initially approached us concerning the possibility of undertaking such an enterprise. It has been a pleasure to collaborate with him and we are mindful of the professional care he has taken with every stage of this venture.

Finally, we express our gratitude to the distinguished Directors of the three borrowing institutions and we trust *Scottish Treasures* brings much pleasure and enjoyment to all visitors to the exhibition.

TIMOTHY CLIFFORD
Director-General, National Galleries of Scotland

Foreword

As Directors of the Memphis Brooks Museum of Art, the Georgia Museum of Art and the New Orleans Museum of Art, we join together to welcome *Scottish Treasures: Masterpieces from the National Gallery of Scotland* to the United States. It is in fact the very first exhibition of paintings from the National Gallery of Scotland to come to this country, and in a very real sense it represents the depth and quality of the collections that are housed at The Mound in Edinburgh.

Replete with masterpieces by some of the most important names in the history of art, it goes without saying that it is a privilege to be able to work with, and bring to our visitors, such an exhibition. For us as Directors, and for our museums, such opportunities are rare. They help us not only with our critically important educational mission, but also with our continual drive to inspire new audiences.

We join together to thank the Trustees and staff of the National Gallery of Scotland for their generosity in making this wonderful exhibition available to us. In particular, we are grateful to Timothy Clifford, Director-General of the National Galleries of Scotland and Michael Clarke, Director of the National Gallery of Scotland. It really is due to their wisdom, foresight and energy that this opportunity has become a reality.

We also are pleased to acknowledge the key role played by David Setford, and ArtReach International, in organizing this exhibition. *Scottish Treasures: Masterpieces from the National Gallery of Scotland* represents ArtReach's first exhibition to come to the USA, and we would like to wish this new and exciting venture the very best for the future.

Finally, we should thank our major underwriters for their local support of this exhibition – in Memphis, The Bodine Company, NewSouth Capital Management, the Brooks Museum League and the *Commercial Appeal*; in Athens, the Director's Circle of the Georgia Museum of Art, the Friends of the Georgia Museum of Art, and the W. Newton Morris Charitable Foundation; and in New Orleans, the Fellows of the New Orleans Museum of Art. Without the generous support and far-sighted commitment to our communities of these organizations, our visitors would not have the opportunity to appreciate the outstanding treasures from the National Gallery of Scotland.

E. JOHN BULLARD
The Montine McDaniel Freeman Director, New Orleans Museum of Art

KAYWIN FELDMAN
Director, the Memphis Brooks Museum of Art

DR WILLIAM U. EILAND
Director, the Georgia Museum of Art

Acknowledgements

After a lengthy gestation period, ArtReach International was finally incorporated on the very same day that my baby daughter was born – June 2, 1999. Its mission is simple – to bring high-quality exhibitions of European art from European museums to American museums. During my almost ten years tenure as Chief Curator at the Norton Museum of Art in West Palm Beach, it had seemed to me that it was in this field that I could really help many fine institutions in the United States.

In those distant and hectic days of last summer, I literally had no idea how my infant enterprise would develop, and what would be ArtReach's first exhibition to reach America. One possibility was a show of works by Albert Marquet from the French national collections held at the Pompidou Center in Paris (a show which will open at the Columbia Museum of Art, Columbia, South Carolina, in October of 2001). At the suggestion of John Bullard, Director of the New Orleans Museum of Art, I wrote to Timothy Clifford, Director-General of the National Galleries of Scotland, suggesting a meeting concerning possible projects. I was delighted to receive an immediate reply from Michael Clarke, Director of the National Gallery of Scotland, indicating not only that he would be glad to see me, but also that he had a specific exhibition proposal in mind! The rest, as they say, is history. I can only say that as the founder of ArtReach, I am immensely gratified, and somewhat overawed, that my very first offering comes from such an illustrious source.

I am deeply grateful to the Trustees of the National Galleries of Scotland and its staff. In particular, I would like to thank Timothy Clifford, Michael Clarke, Janis Adams, Anne Buddle and Sheila Scott for their trust, generosity and patience.

Without the American museums there would have been no tour, so I must thank the directors and staff of the Memphis Brooks Museum of Art, the Georgia Museum of Art, and the New Orleans Museum of Art. In particular, I have already mentioned John Bullard's important role; I must also thank Kaywin Feldman and Dr William Eiland for their foresight and commitment to this important project.

John Pritchard in London and Peter Dunston in Rhode Island have, in their different but equally important ways, both been driving forces behind the foundation and development of ArtReach. I must also thank my wife, Lindsay, and my daughter, Verity, who were my inspiration over the last eighteen months, and who have put up with my frequent and often long absences

DAVID F. SETFORD
Director, ArtReach International

Introduction

It seems peculiarly fitting that, for this tour to the United States of an exhibition of paintings from the National Gallery of Scotland, we should be including our great Frederic Edwin Church of *Niagara Falls from the American Side* (no.50). This masterpiece of American painting was a distinguished visitor to British shores when it was exhibited in London in 1868 and evoked favourable comparison with the great J. M.W. Turner. Eventually it made its home in Scotland when it was presented in 1887 to the recently founded National Gallery of Scotland by John Stewart Kennedy (1830–1909), an émigré Scot who had made his fortune in the States as a railroad commission merchant and private banker, and whose largesse also extended to many of the great institutions of his adopted country, including the New York Public Library and the Metropolitan Museum of Art.

Church's spectacular landscape, which is almost cinematic in its scope and grandeur, arrived in Edinburgh thirty-seven years after the foundation stone of the National Gallery of Scotland had been laid by Prince Albert, the Prince Consort, on 30 August 1850. Queen Victoria, whose own love of Scotland was almost as important as the novels of Sir Walter Scott in promoting the burgeoning Scottish tourist industry, tactfully absented herself from the event. It was indeed a major milestone in the establishment of a proper sense of nationhood in a country whose fortunes had been constitutionally tied to those of its more powerful neighbour, England, since the Act of Union of 1707, by which the Parliaments of the two countries had been united. A Scottish Parliament, with certain powers devolved from London , was finally re-instituted in 1999 and now sits in its temporary home, Free Church College, Edinburgh, overlooking the National Gallery of Scotland. Both buildings were designed by the same architect, William Henry Playfair (1790–1857). Free Church or 'New' College was built in the Gothic style, as befits its original and main purpose; the National Gallery in the classical style, reflecting its designation as a 'temple of the arts'.

The Gallery finally opened to the public in 1859 and originally shared its premises with the Royal Scottish Academy, Scotland's senior artists' association – the equivalent of the London Royal Academy – and with which it co-habited until 1910–11. Further building work at that time in the National Gallery meant that the Academy removed to the neo-classical building immediately in front of the National Gallery, the former Royal Institution building, henceforth known as the Royal Scottish Academy building. This, too, had been designed by Playfair and its construction is recorded in this exhibition in Alexander Nasmyth's wonderful painting of 1825 (no.38). Nasmyth's panoramic view also reinforces Edinburgh's status at the heart of the Scottish Enlightenment and illustrates how, with its superb classical architecture, it came to be known as the 'Athens of the North'.

Many of the works of art displayed in the northern capital of Britain were, of course, Scottish, and pictures of the national school, which developed different traditions distinct from those south of the border, featured prominently on the walls of the National Gallery in the nineteenth century. In the previous century Allan Ramsay (no.34) had emerged as one of the most refined and educated of all European portraitists. Whereas Ramsay was widely travelled, and had studied in France and Italy, and settled in London, Sir Henry Raeburn established his portrait practice in Edinburgh (no.37) and recorded many of the great figures of the Enlightenment. The nineteenth century saw the institutionalisation of art and its teaching and works by many of the major artists who were members of the Royal Scottish Academy were acquired for the national collection. .

Of course, the European schools have also been well represented in the National Gallery since its inception and early masterpieces which entered the collection included an outstanding group of French eighteenth-century pictures from the Lady Murray of Henderland bequest of 1861. Other gifts have comprised Mrs Nisbet Hamilton Ogilvy of Biel's bequest of twenty-eight pictures in 1921, and the 11th Marquess of Lothian's bequest of eighteen works in 1941. Twenty-one Impressionist and Post-Impressionist paintings came in Sir Alexander Maitland's gift of 1960 and bequest of 1965. The

Gallery received it first official purchase grant in 1903 of £3,000 annually. This has obviously grown considerably since then and a whole host of masterpieces have been acquired. Mention should also be made of the magnificent Sutherland Loan, initially of twenty-nine paintings and including masterpieces by Raphael, Rembrandt and Titian, which arrived in the Gallery in 1945 and continues to the present day.

As the collection grew over the years – it now numbers some 1500 paintings and sculptures and nearly 20,000 works of art on paper – the question of space became paramount. Reference has already been made to the 1910–11 enlargement of the National Gallery of Scotland. Sister galleries also sprang up in Edinburgh. The Scottish National Portrait Gallery opened in Queen Street in 1889 and, considerably later, the Scottish National Gallery of Modern Art was established in 1960, at first in Inverleith House in the Botanic Gardens, before it relocated in 1984 to its permanent home in the former John Watson's College in the West End of Edinburgh. As recently as 1999 the modern gallery received a new partner in the shape of the Dean Gallery, which concentrates on our splendid Surrealist and Dada collections. All these Galleries fall under one umbrella organisation, the National Galleries of Scotland, reporting to one Board of Trustees and Director General and sharing central departments such as Conservation, Registration and Development. The main funding of the National Galleries is through government taxes, though extensive sums are raised externally for purchases of works of art and for capital projects.

Our current major initiative is the 'Playfair Project', named after the Gallery's original architect. This scheme involves the creation of a whole suite of facilities currently lacking in the National Gallery of Scotland, including a lecture theatre, an education suite, information technology access, an enlarged bookshop, and a restaurant and cafeteria. These will all be provided in the planned underground link between the National Gallery and the neighbouring Royal Scottish Academy building, illustrated below. Furthermore, the Academy's magnificent exhibition spaces will be thoroughly renovated and provide an exhibition venue worthy to stand alongside the finest in the world. At present large parts of the permanent collection in the National Gallery have to be taken down whenever we wish to accommodate a major exhibition, as is currently the case with our major show for 2001, *Rembrandt's Women*. The future availability of top-class exhibition space in the Royal Scottish Academy will solve this problem.

Britain has seen many highly successful museum projects in the last few years, such as the Great Court of the British Museum, the Neptune Court at the National Maritime Museum, the central court of the Wallace Collection and, most distinctive and impressive of all, the creation of Tate Modern at Bankside. These achievements have all been in London, however. Scotland may have been twenty-six years later than England (1824) in establishing its own National Gallery, but we are confident that the Playfair Project will soon take its place as one of the most significant and welcome museum developments of the new millennium. Completion is scheduled for 2005 and represents the next major chapter in the history of the National Gallery of Scotland.

MICHAEL CLARKE
Director, National Gallery of Scotland

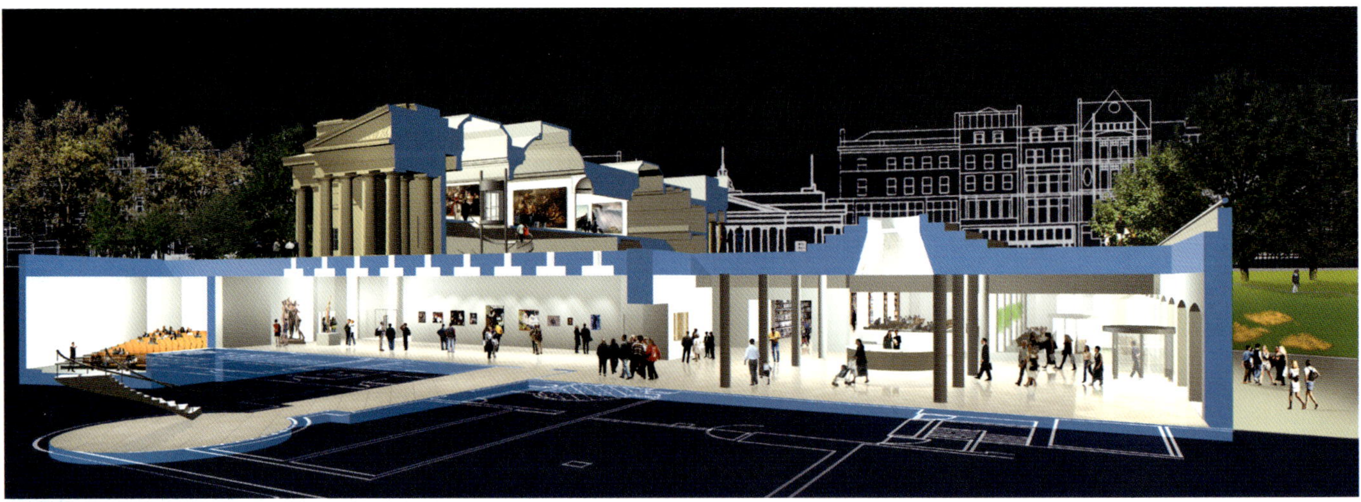

CATALOGUE

The entries are divided into national schools within which the works are placed in approximate chronological order of execution. Measurements are given height preceding width.

Attributed to the Workshop of Andrea del Verrocchio *c.*1435–1488

1 *The Virgin Adoring the Christ Child ('The Ruskin Madonna')*, *c.*1470–80

Tempera (and oil?) on canvas, transferred from panel · 42 × 30in (106.7 × 76.3cm)
Purchased with the aid of the National Art Collections Fund and the Pilgrim Trust 1975
NG 2338

The popular title of this painting records the fact that it was among the prized possessions of the influential nineteenth-century English critic and artist John Ruskin (1819–1900), who recalled: 'I bought it for a hundred pounds out of the Manfrini Palace at Venice; and consider it an entirely priceless painting, exemplary for all time.'

The picture is not in good condition, the paint layer having been transferred from its original wooden support to canvas and extensively restored. It nevertheless displays some remarkable features, notably the grandiose backdrop of classical architecture, which is exceptional in Florentine Madonna compositions of this period. The receding lines of the pavement follow a precise perspective grid incised directly into the gesso ground layer and still visible on the surface. These incisions extend beneath the figures of the Virgin and Child, whose principal contours were also indented with a stylus, presumably from a cartoon (full-scale drawing). The ruined architecture may have been meant to represent the Roman Temple of Peace, which according to legend collapsed at the moment of Christ's birth – a clear visual metaphor for the triumph of the new religion over the old. Christ's action of placing a finger in his mouth was probably intended as a reference to the Incarnation, Christ as the Word made flesh. The gesture carries this meaning more explicitly in similar images by Verrocchio's contemporaries Fra Filippo Lippi (*c.*1406–1469) and Andrea della Robbia (1435–1525). Indeed, it was the equivalent figures in Lippi's altarpiece of the *Adoration of the Christ Child*, painted in the late 1450s for the chapel in the Palazzo Medici-Riccardi in Florence (and now in the Gemäldegalerie, Berlin), which served as the direct compositional model for the *Ruskin Madonna*. Fifteenth-century viewers would have understood the translucent veil upon which Jesus reclines both as a representation of the infant's swaddling clothes and an allusion to the winding cloth of his future Passion. Such details explain the introspective, devotional attitude of the Virgin, who has just become aware of her son's momentous fate.

The authorship of the *Ruskin Madonna* has been much debated, although it is generally agreed to date from the 1470s. It was ascribed to Filippo Lippi at the time of its acquisition by Ruskin, but most scholars since then have attributed it to Verrocchio, or to a member of his studio, largely on the basis of comparison with his sculpted reliefs (few undisputed paintings by him survive). Verrocchio was one of the most brilliant and versatile artists of his day who practised initially as a goldsmith but diversified into sculpture and painting in the 1460s. He ran a busy workshop and regularly delegated work on major commissions to his assistants, Leonardo da Vinci and Lorenzo di Credi among them.

More recently, the suggestion that the *Ruskin Madonna* might be the work of the young Domenico Ghirlandaio (1448/9–1494), who probably trained under Alesso Baldovinetti but was certainly influenced by Verrocchio, has gained some support. The picture has been linked on stylistic grounds with four other Madonna compositions (in the National Gallery of Art, Washington; the Louvre, Paris; the monastery at Camaldoli in Tuscany; and the Metropolitan Museum of Art, New York), none of which, however, can be attributed to Ghirlandaio with any certainty (for these paintings see H. Brigstocke, *Italian and Spanish Paintings in the National Gallery of Scotland*, Edinburgh, 1993, pp.202–4, figs.68–71).

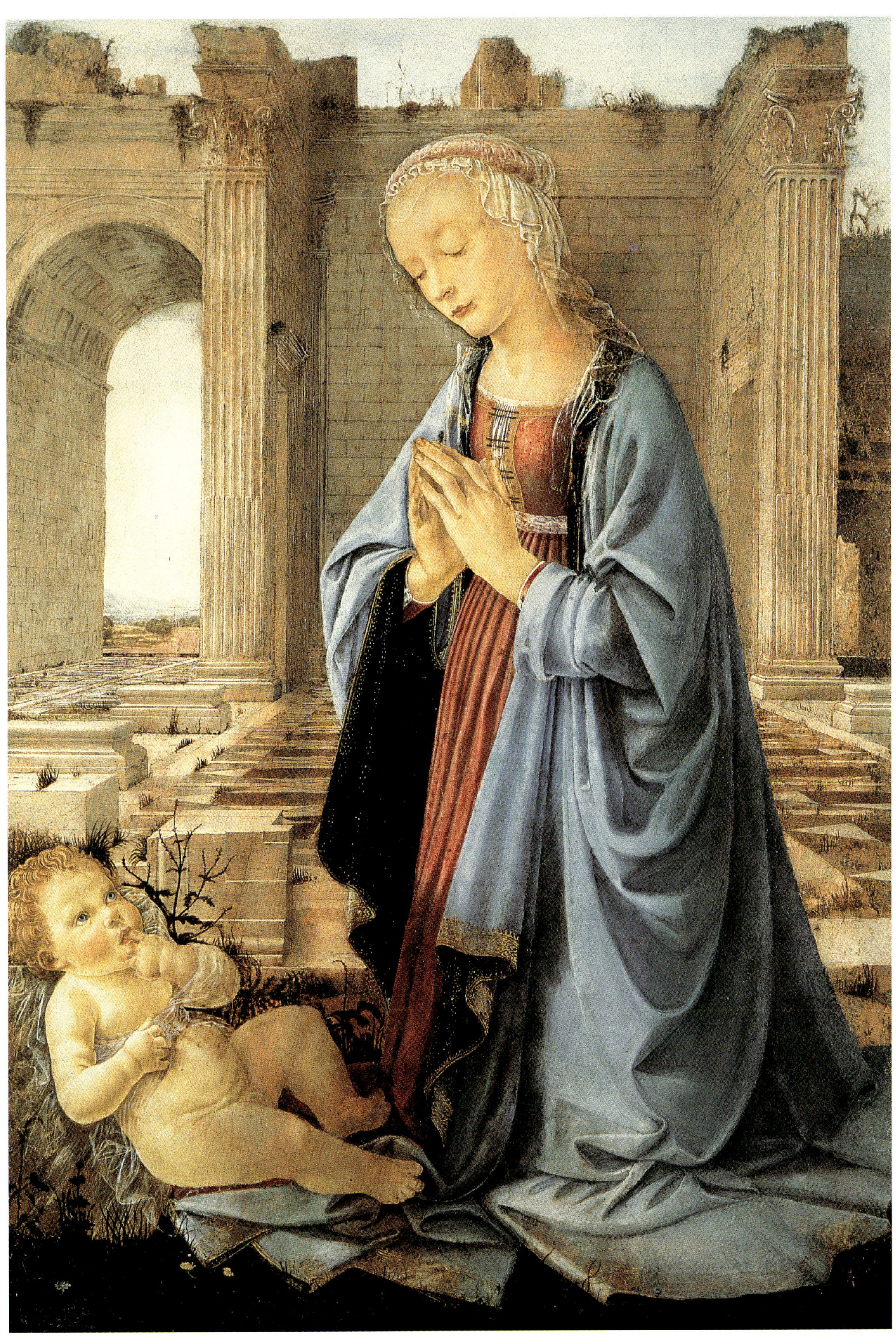

Pietro Vannucci, called Perugino *c.*1450–1523

2 *Four Male Nudes*, *c.*1500–10

Canvas · 28⅞ x 21⅞in (73.3 x 55.5cm)
Presented by the National Art Collections Fund 1934
NG 1805

This painting is a fragment of a larger composition, the subject of which has not been established. It was once given the fanciful title 'The Court of Apollo' – presumably on account of the fact that one of the figures has a lyre, an instrument closely associated with Apollo, but by no means exclusive to him. Given that the men are shown almost or completely naked, the subject must have been either a mythological one or, perhaps more likely, a secular allegory. The fragment almost certainly comes from the lower left corner of the composition, and assuming that the design was balanced and had a central vanishing point, the perspective lines of the pavement can be used to calculate a putative width of approximately 180 cm for the original canvas. The two figures in the middle appear to gaze past the pillar to a central focus of interest, and both make gestures of humility or adoration. The nude at the right, on the other hand, looks upwards.

Perugino was an extremely productive artist who in his maturity maintained workshops in both Florence and Perugia, but secular subjects of this kind are rare in his work. He is known to have painted some mythological frescoes (destroyed) in 1490 at Lorenzo de' Medici's Villa Spedaletto near Volterra, and a large painting of *Mars and Venus in the Net of Vulcan* was in his studio at the time of his death. Of his surviving secular works, the present painting has most in common with the *Combat between Love and Chastity*, now in the Louvre, Paris. Completed in 1505, this was Perugino's contribution to the celebrated series of canvases commissioned by Isabella d'Este, Marchioness of Mantua, to decorate her private study in the Castello di San Giorgio in Mantua. The *Four Male Nudes* is painted on the same fine-weave canvas as the Louvre painting, and both the rather dry handling and the figure scale are similar; it is accordingly usually dated to the same moment in Perugino's career.

Born at Città della Pieve in Umbria, Perugino enjoyed considerable success from relatively early in his career, including a summons to Rome in 1481 to take charge of the decoration of the upper walls of the newly completed Sistine Chapel. The sweetness, grace and serenity of his devotional paintings were especially admired and had an enormous influence throughout Italy, not least on his own pupil Raphael. By the time this canvas was painted it is probably true to say that Perugino was still the most sought-after painter in Italy, although by then his manner was distinctly old-fashioned when compared to the innovative styles being introduced by Leonardo da Vinci, Michelangelo and Giorgione.

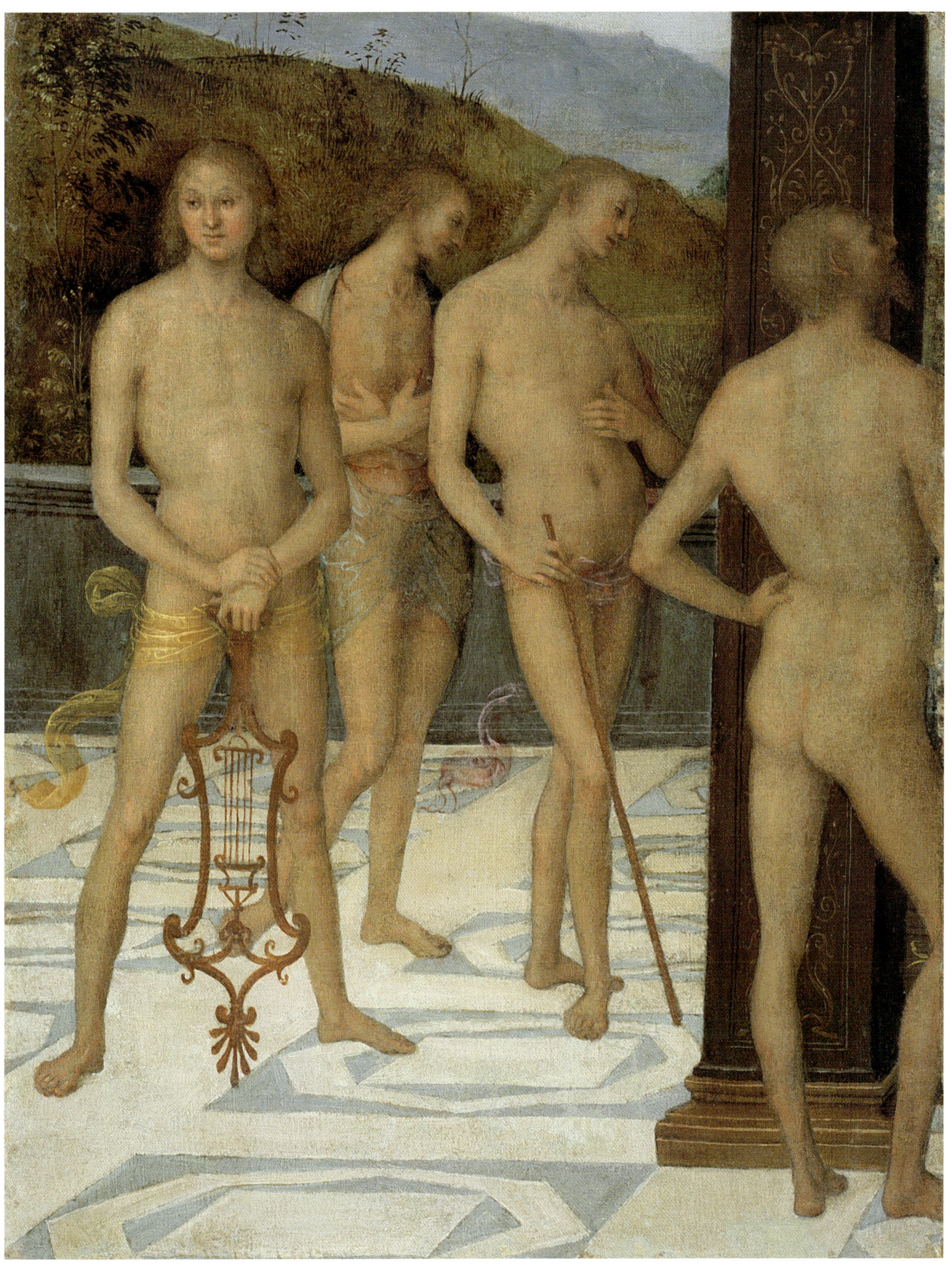

Paris Bordon 1500–1571

3 *The Rest on the Return from Egypt*, c.1540–50

Oil on canvas · 41 × 55½in (104 × 140.8cm)
Accepted in lieu of tax from the Estate of Colonel W.J. Stirling of Keir
and allocated to the National Gallery of Scotland, with a contribution from Gallery funds 1996
NG 2651

This is a fine and characteristic work by Bordon, probably dating from the 1540s. In the seventeenth century it was in the possession of the patrician Venier family, and was described in glowing terms by the Venetian writer on art Marco Boschini in *La carta del navegar pitoresco* of 1660 (G. Canova, *Paris Bordon*, Venice, 1964, p.81). It represents the Holy Family resting on their return journey to the Holy Land following their exile in Egypt, and includes the legendary episode of the first meeting of the infants Christ and St John the Baptist. The foreground is dominated by the reclining figure of Mary, who seems absorbed in thought, reflecting on a passage of scripture she has been reading, while in the middle distance Joseph can be seen watering the donkey at a stream. Perhaps the most striking feature of the painting is the panoramic landscape vista of wooded hills and valleys stretching to distant mountains. Similar landscapes seen from a high viewpoint appear in numerous other paintings from Bordon's maturity. Many of these share with the present composition a pronounced disparity of scale between the monumental foreground figures and the diminutive landscape forms in the background with which they are directly juxtaposed, with little in the way of progressive gradation of scale through the middle distance. The ruddy flesh tones, fussily folded, faceted draperies and rather formulaic outlining of the foreground plants are all hallmarks of Bordon's style.

Bordon was an artist who frequently recycled figures and compositions, and the pose of the Virgin in this painting reappears on a slightly larger scale in a *Holy Family with St John the Baptist in an Extensive Landscape* formerly in the Ellesmere Collection (Canova 1964, p.77). An exact copy of the Edinburgh composition in an Italian private collection appears to be at best a workshop replica, although it has been attributed to Bordon himself. (V. Sgarbi, 'Note su Paris Bordon' in *Paris Bordon e il suo tempo: Atti del convegno internazionale di studi, Treviso, 28–30 October 1985*, Treviso, 1987, p.172).

Born at Treviso on the Venetian mainland, Bordon (or Bordone) is recorded as a painter in Venice in 1518, where he was probably a pupil of Titian. His name features in a list of members of the *Fraglia* (the Venetian painters' guild) begun in 1530. Apart from trips to Milan, Augsburg and possibly Fontainebleau, he spent most of his career working in Venice and in his native Treviso. He was one of the Venetian painters most receptive to the elaborate and artificial *maniera* style imported from central Italy, of which he developed his own distinctive variation. In addition to the usual repertoire of subjects, Bordon made a speciality of mildly erotic secular paintings featuring buxom, often bare-breasted women with elaborate coiffures, of a type first popularised in the 1510s by Titian and Palma Vecchio. The National Gallery of Scotland also owns a fine work of this kind by the artist, *Venetian Women at their Toilet* (Brigstocke 1993, pp.36–7).

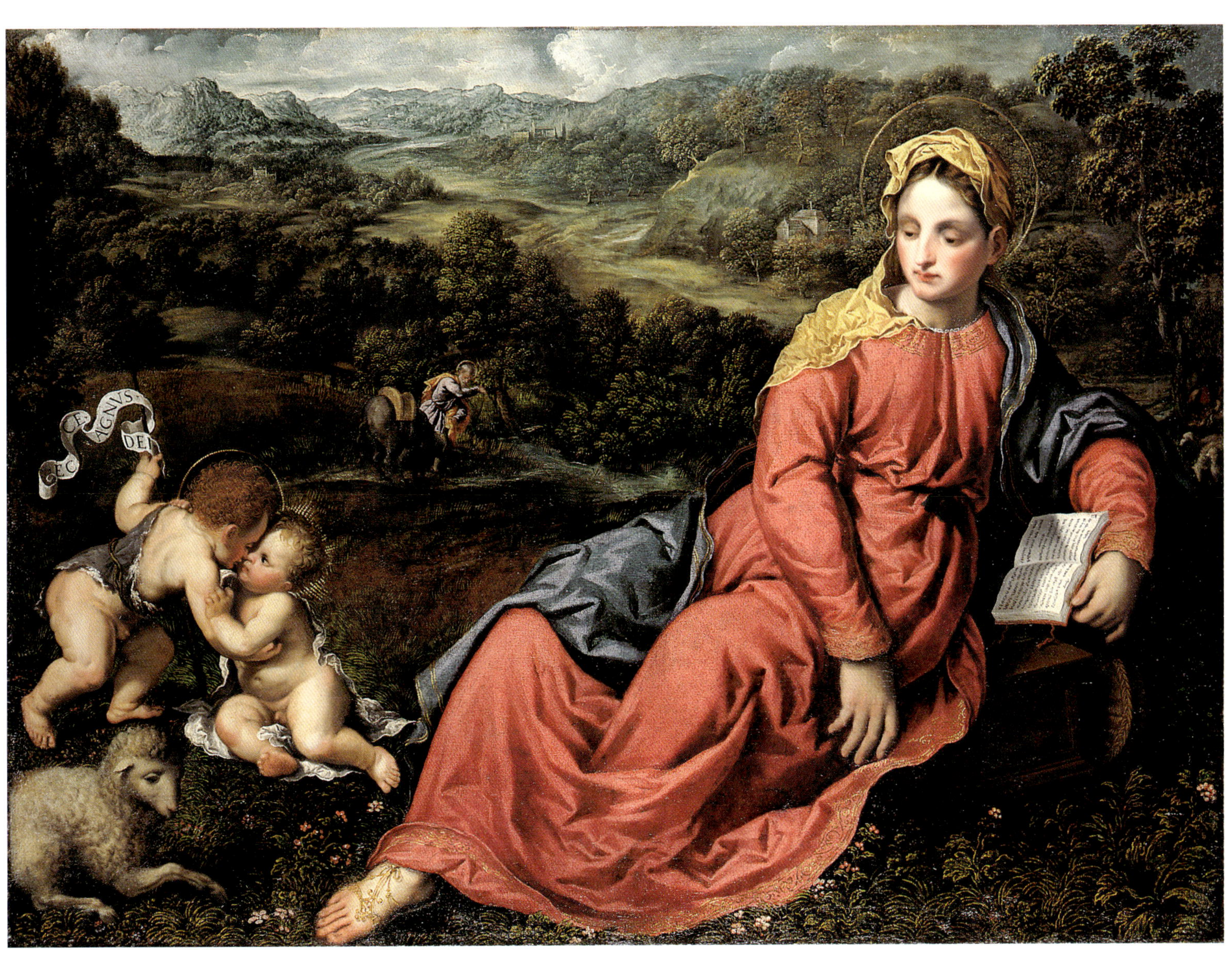
EC CE AGNVS DEI

Paolo Veronese 1528–1588

4 *Venus, Mars and Cupid*, c.1580

Oil on canvas · 65 × 49¾in (165.2 × 126.5)
Purchased by the Royal Institution 1859; transferred to the National Gallery of Scotland 1868
NG 339

Paolo Caliari trained and established his reputation in his native Verona in the 1540s. By the early 1550s he was receiving major commissions from Venice, and in 1553 he moved there definitively and was known as 'Veronese' after his birthplace. Assisted by his brother and later by his sons, his highly productive workshop became the principal rival in Venice to that of Tintoretto. He won major decorative commissions for the church of San Sebastiano and the Ducal Palace, and gained the support of a network of wealthy Venetian patricians. A series of vast banquet scenes for monastic refectories, one of which elicited the censure of the Inquisition and led to a fascinating court hearing, are among his most famous works. Veronese also worked in fresco, notably at the Villa Barbaro at Maser. The last decade of his career was especially productive and included, for the first time, important orders from abroad. A superb colourist, Veronese's paintings are typically filled with exotic figures, sumptuous fabrics, grandiose architecture and much incidental detail.

In this late work of about 1580, Venus gently comforts her son Cupid, who has been frightened by a lively little spaniel. This seemingly whimsical intrusion of an everyday incident into a mythological subject adds a note of humour and may have triggered other associations. As a traditional symbol of marital fidelity, the appearance of a lap dog in a painting of the adulterous relationship between Venus (who was married to Vulcan) and Mars (who has begun to undress her) could hardly be less appropriate – a neat inversion on the part of the artist. Perhaps this is why the dog is so agitated. Alternatively, the dog, which appears almost to ravish the startled Cupid, might symbolise the carnal passions. The goddess of love is perched somewhat awkwardly on Mars' knee. He is poorly integrated into the composition, and since he does not feature in Veronese's otherwise closely related sheet of preparatory sketches in the British Museum, London, he may have been inserted at a relatively late stage, possibly by an assistant. The execution of Venus, Cupid and the spaniel is on a par with Veronese's best late works, and refutes the recent suggestion that the painting is entirely the work of his son Carletto (see *The Art of Paolo Veronese*, exhibition catalogue, National Gallery of Art, Washington, 1988–9, pp.136–7, under cat.no.70). The tonal imbalance of the painting (more pronounced now than it was originally) is due to a technical peculiarity, the figures of Venus and Cupid alone having been prepared with a thick, white ground layer, which guaranteed the luminosity of their flesh. The very sketchy treatment of Cupid's wings indicates that the painting may have been left unfinished.

It has recently been established that this painting is probably identical with one presented as a diplomatic gift by the Spanish Crown to Charles I when Prince of Wales, during his ill-judged trip to Spain in 1623 to win the hand in marriage of the Spanish Infanta (S. Walker Schroth, 'Charles I, the duque de Lerma and Veronese's Edinburgh *Mars and Venus*', *Burlington Magazine*, CXXXIX, 1997, pp.548–50).

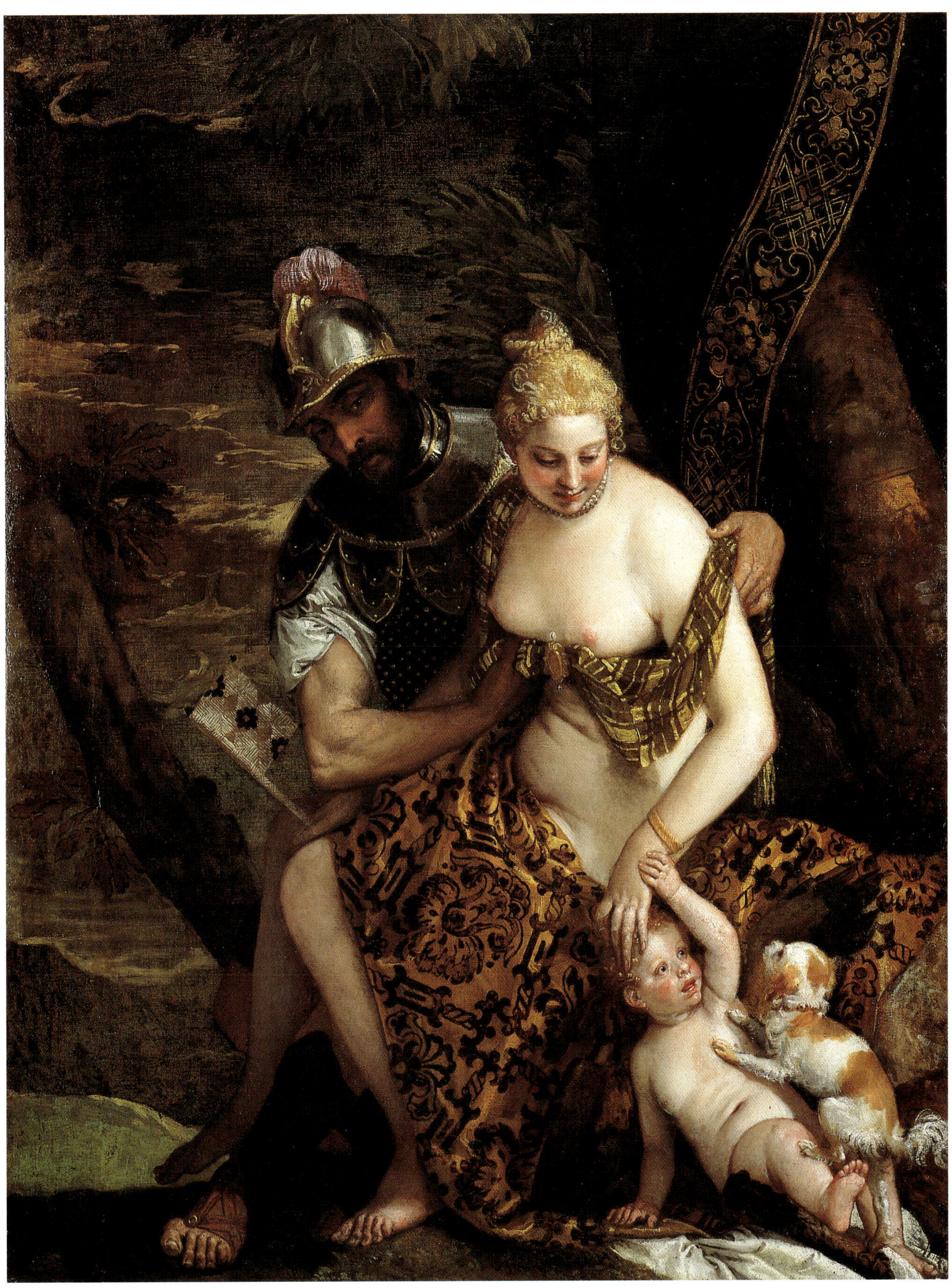

Domenico Zampieri, called Domenichino 1581–1641

5 *The Adoration of the Shepherds*, c.1606–8

Oil on canvas · 56¼ × 45¼in (143 × 115cm)
Purchased 1971
NG 2313

Domenichino was born in Bologna and trained there under Denys Calvaert and then in the Carracci Academy. In 1602 he moved to Rome and became a favoured assistant to Annibale Carracci. He was the leading exponent of the more restrained, classical tendency in Italian painting of the earlier seventeenth century, characterised by ordered, easily legible compositions and clearly articulated gestures and expressions. He enjoyed considerable success in Rome and Bologna before moving to Naples in 1631.

The nocturnal setting of this *Adoration*, with the entire scene bathed in brilliant divine light emanating from the infant Jesus at the centre, is derived ultimately from the celebrated altarpiece by Correggio known as *La Notte* (Gemäldegalerie, Dresden), then in the church of San Prospero in Reggio Emilia. A close-knit group of angels and gesticulating shepherds look on in wonder, while the shepherd at the left sounds what must have been a startlingly loud celebratory blast on his bagpipes.

Although the attribution of the painting is not in question, its exact status is problematic. The usually reliable Giovan Pietro Bellori, author of *Le vite de' pittori, scultori ed architetti moderni*, published in Rome in 1672, gave an accurate description of its composition in his biography of Annibale Carracci. He stated that he did not know the whereabouts of Carracci's painting, but that a copy of it by Domenichino had been taken to France at an unspecified date. This is an entirely plausible scenario, for Domenichino made copies and variants of several other works by Carracci while working as his assistant. However, the surviving evidence indicates that on this occasion Bellori may have been mistaken, and that the design of the Edinburgh painting is essentially Domenichino's own, albeit indebted in many respects to several different nativity compositions by Carracci. Quite apart from the fact that the figure types are more characteristic of Domenichino than Annibale, strong support for this assertion is furnished by the existence of a preparatory drawing by Domenichino himself for the figure of Joseph carrying a bundle of hay in the background, and another more loosely related to the bagpiper (both in the Royal Library, Windsor Castle), which would clearly have been superfluous were he replicating an existing composition. A possible source of Bellori's confusion is the existence of a quite similar painting by Carracci (Musée des Beaux-Arts, Orléans), which passed from the Ludovisi collection in Rome to that of Everard Jabach in Paris around 1650. The latter painting was certainly one of Domenichino's main sources for his composition. He would also have known Annibale's etching of the *Adoration of the Shepherds* of 1606, and evidently drew further ideas from a group of Carracci drawings on this theme (Pierpont Morgan Library, New York; private collection), one of them usually attributed to Annibale's brother Agostino (J. Paul Getty Museum, Los Angeles). A life study by Annibale for the kneeling boy holding a dove (Royal Library, Windsor Castle) seems to have been made explicitly to assist his pupil, a practice of which there are other examples. Finally, a crude etching by Stephan Colbenschlag (1591–after 1653), published in Rome, reproduces the Edinburgh painting in reverse (with some minor omissions) and credits its design to Domenichino.

Given the multiplicity of sources upon which he drew, Domenichino's composition is remarkable for its structural coherence and clarity. Dating from about 1606–8, the picture may have been painted in a spirit of friendly rivalry with his fellow pupils Giovanni Lanfranco and Sisto Badalocchio, both of whom produced nocturnal nativity scenes at about the same date which are similarly indebted to Annibale Carracci.

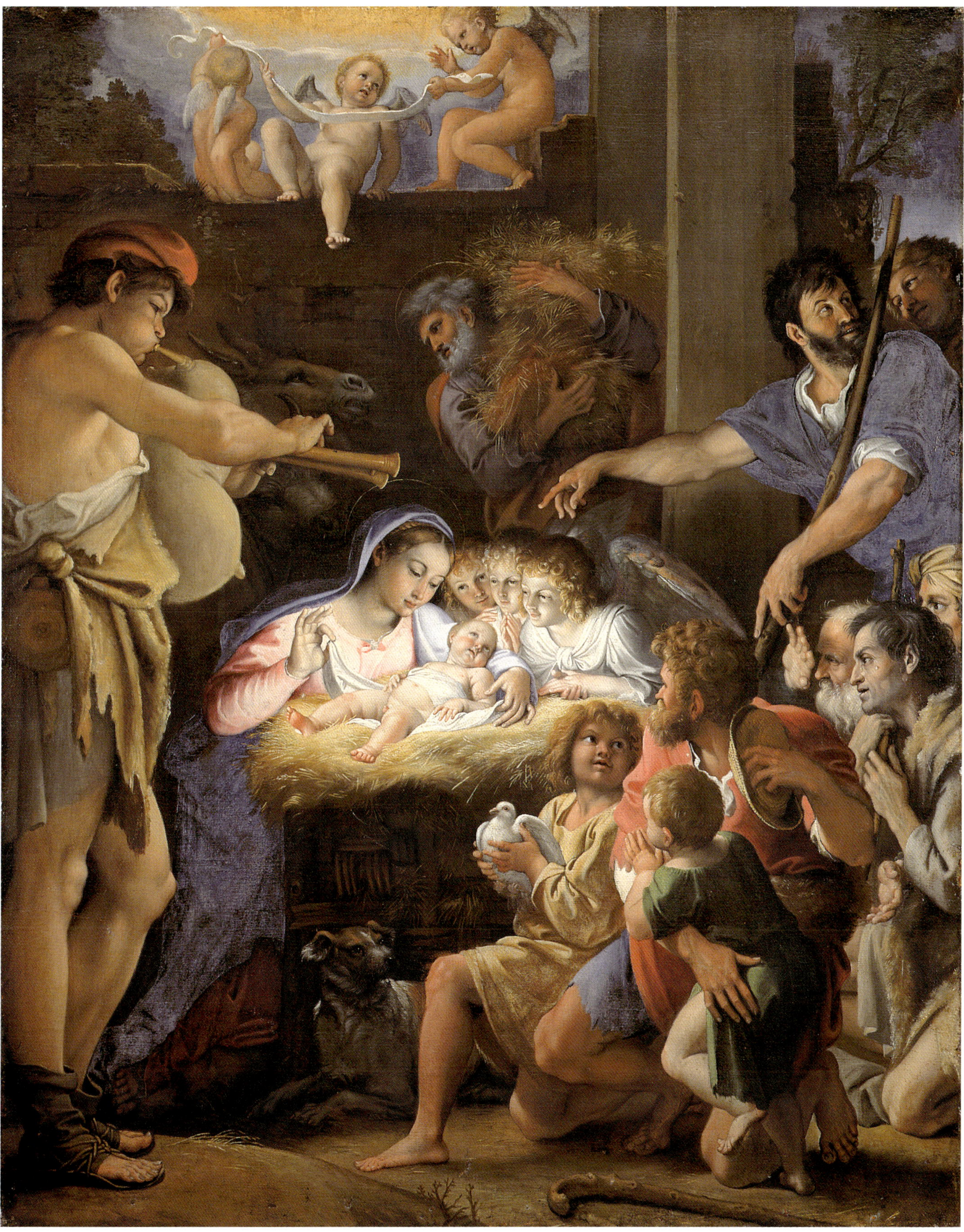

Giulio Cesare Procaccini 1574–1625

6 *The Raising of the Cross*, c.1615–20

Oil on canvas · 85¾ × 58½in (218 × 148.6cm)
Purchased 1965
NG 2276

Born in Bologna, Procaccini moved with his family to Milan as a boy, where he was trained by his father and elder brothers. Having been active initially as a sculptor, he turned to painting around 1600 and became one of the leading Milanese artists of the first quarter of the seventeenth century. Later in his career he also worked in Genoa, where he was influenced by Rubens's paintings, and for the court of Savoy in Turin. Procaccini's style, which was strongly rooted in the late sixteenth-century Milanese tradition, shows little in the way of consistent development over the course of his career.

The Raising of the Cross combines passages of gruesome realism with a highly contrived, densely packed composition full of energy, emotion and flashes of brilliant colour. The design hinges on the dramatically receding diagonal of Christ's tortured body on the cross. The way in which the viewer is confronted very directly with the heightened emotion and violence of the scene is characteristic of religious art produced in Milan under the reformist Archbishop Cardinal Federico Borromeo, who was assiduous in implementing the decrees of the Council of Trent relating to religious images and wrote a book on the subject (*De Pictura Sacra*, Milan, 1624).

The Raising of the Cross has been associated with four other scenes from the Passion of Christ by Procaccini of similar dimensions and style, and there may once have been more: a *Capture of Christ* (private collection; formerly with Piero Corsini, Inc., New York); a *Flagellation* (Museum of Fine Arts, Boston); a *Crowning with Thorns* (Graves Art Gallery, Sheffield); and an *Ecce Homo* (Dallas Museum of Art) which, however, is significantly larger than the other canvases (for these paintings see M. Rosci, *Giulio Cesare Procaccini*, Soncino, 1993, pp.42–5, 108–11). The original location of this hypothetical ensemble is not known, but an oratory belonging to a lay confraternity dedicated to the Passion is a possibility. All the canvases appear to date from about 1615 to 1620. More problematic is the suggestion that the series may have included a *Baptism of Christ* (National Gallery of Slovakia, Bratislava), again of similar style and dimensions but featuring a less cramped composition than the other paintings (L. Konečný, 'Due segnalazioni per Giulio Cesare Procaccini', *Paragone (Arte)*, XXXVII, 441, 1986, pp.59–64). If so, the theme of the series must have been the broader one of the life of Christ rather than just his Passion.

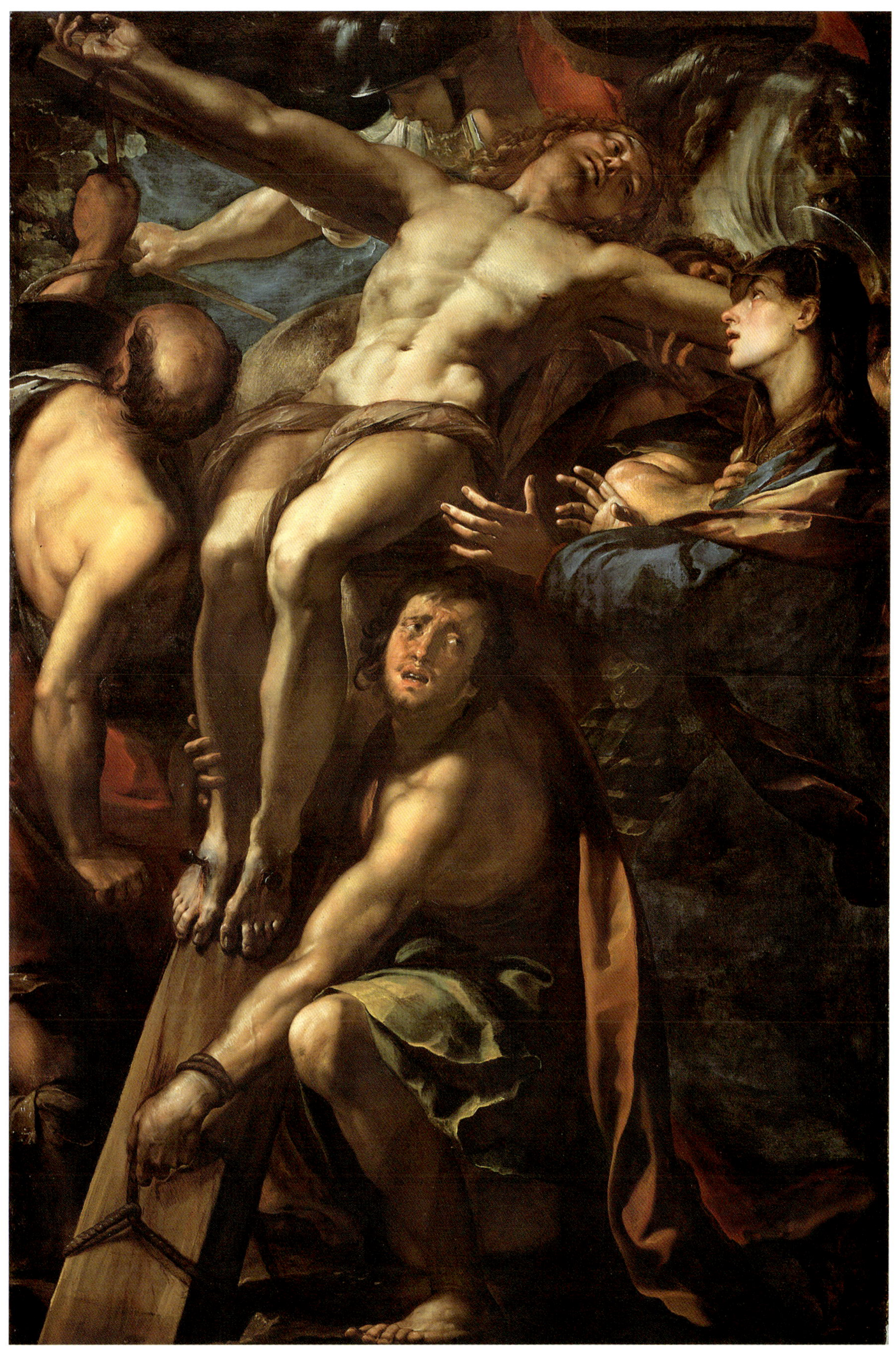

Giovanni Francesco Barbieri, called Guercino 1591–1666

7 *The Penitent St Peter*, 1639

Oil on canvas · 40¾ × 33¾in (103.7 × 85.8cm)
Purchased by the Royal Institution 1831; transferred to the National Gallery of Scotland 1858
NG 39

Guercino was born in the town of Cento between Bologna and Ferrara and, with the exception of two years spent in Rome (1621–3), he lived there until 1642, when he moved his studio to Bologna following the death of his rival Guido Reni. He was largely self-taught, developing a highly original, naturalistic manner of painting, which he progressively modified following his visit to Rome in order to conform to the more classical tastes then in vogue. Guercino had an enormously productive and successful career and was one of the greatest draughtsmen of the seventeenth century.

On the evening of Christ's arrest, the apostle Peter three times denied that he knew him in order to save himself. After his third denial a cock crowed, thus fulfilling Christ's prophecy made earlier that day, and on realising this, Peter 'wept bitterly' (Matthew 26: 69–75). Guercino conceived Peter's repentance as almost desperate in its sincerity and intensity. Isolated in a sombre setting, he gazes ardently heavenward with tears streaming down both cheeks and his hands clenched in prayer. The church in the left background alludes to Christ's charge to Peter and his ministry as first bishop of Rome: 'You are Peter, the Rock; and on this rock I will build my church' (Matthew 16: 18). The subject was a popular one in Counter-Reformation Italy as an example of penitence and a warning against weak resolve and betrayal.

This painting is almost certainly identical with a *St Peter* commissioned in 1639 by Cardinal Ciriaco Rocci, Papal Legate of Ferrara, for which a payment of 55 *scudi* is recorded in Guercino's account book on 4 April of that year (B. Ghelfi and Sir D. Mahon (eds.), *Il libro dei conti del Guercino, 1629–1666*, Bologna, 1997, p.96). This was the artist's standard price for a half-length, life-size figure. In his biography of Guercino, Carlo Cesare Malvasia clarified that the saint in Rocci's picture was shown weeping (*Felsina Pittrice*, Bologna, 1678, II, p.364). While still in the artist's studio, the painting was admired by a certain Fra Gioseffo, who recommended to an unnamed correspondent that, provided Guercino were agreeable, he might commission a workshop copy of it. This may be the good quality copy now in the Palazzo Venezia, Rome (see M. Helston and T. Henry, *Guercino in Britain: Paintings from British Collections*, exhibition catalogue, National Gallery, London, 1991, pp.48–9, cat.no.22).

Cardinal Rocci clearly liked Guercino's work, for he also commissioned a *Lucretia*, a *Mary Magdalen* and a *St Paul* from him, and was presented with a *Dead Christ Mourned by the Virgin Mary* by the town council of Cento. He probably acquired his taste for Guercino's art some twenty years previously while serving as Vice-Legate of Ferrara under Cardinal Jacopo Serra, who was the artist's most important early patron.

A preparatory pen and ink sketch for the Edinburgh painting is in the Teylers Museum, Haarlem (*Guercino (1591–1666): Drawings from Dutch Collections*, exhibition catalogue, Teylers Museum, Haarlem, 1991, pp.106–7, cat.no.40). Two other paintings of *The Penitent St Peter* by Guercino are known, one earlier (*c*.1624–5, formerly with Piero Corsini, Inc., New York), the other later (1650, Cassa di Risparmio, Bologna). The former may be identical with a *St Peter* by Guercino listed in a 1633 inventory of the Ludovisi collection in Rome.

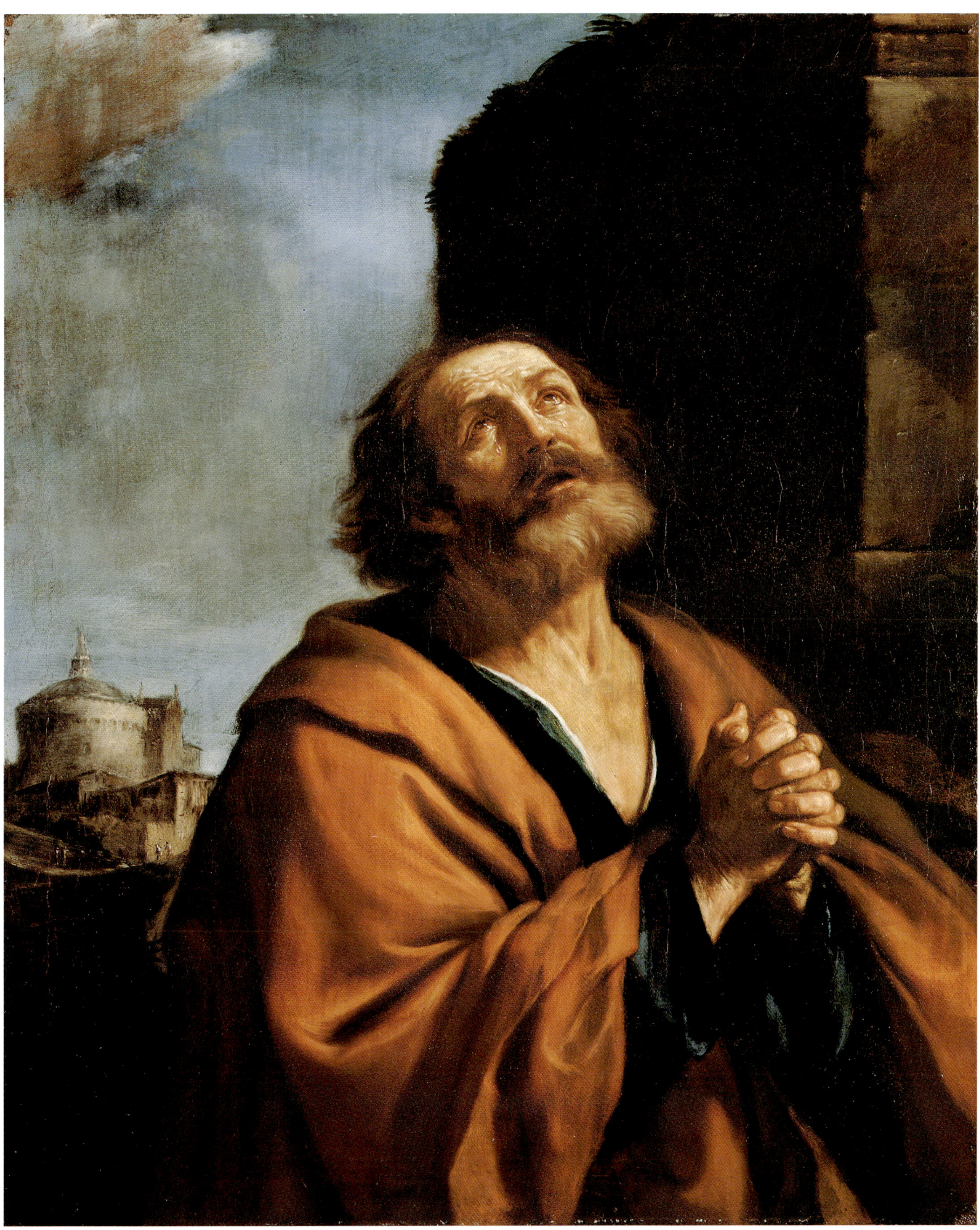

Guido Reni 1575–1642

8 *The Infant Moses with Pharaoh's Crown*, c.1640

Oil on canvas · 52 × 68in (132.2 × 172.7cm)
Purchased 1979
NG 2375

Guido Reni was probably the most successful and sought-after Italian painter of the first half of the seventeenth century, despite being notoriously difficult and temperamental. Like Domenichino, he trained in his native Bologna first with Calvaert and then in the Carracci Academy. He established his reputation in Rome, where he was resident from 1601 to 1614, and thereafter was based mainly in Bologna, executing commissions for the most elevated patrons in Italy and abroad. His paintings display an unfailing sense of grace and elegance combined, in all but his last works, with a powerful naturalism in the depiction of forms and textures. Towards the end of his life Reni produced a group of canvases using a restricted palette of mainly pastel shades and a sketchy, seemingly unfinished technique, of which this *Infant Moses with Pharaoh's Crown* is an excellent example. Reni's biographer Carlo Cesare Malvasia (*Felsina Pittrice*, Bologna, 1678), who admired the artist greatly and is an invaluable source of information about his life and work, was nevertheless ambivalent about this 'second manner'. He attributed the seemingly hurried, slapdash technique of the late paintings to Reni's desperate attempts to raise money quickly to pay off debts arising from his addiction to gambling.

Although an overall descriptive economy and lack of finish are a central feature of Reni's late style, it seems likely that this painting is genuinely unfinished (*abbozzato* or 'blocked-out', to use a contemporary term). The warm brown ground which Reni applied to the canvas before commencing his composition is left clearly visible over quite large areas, and not only in those places where it serves for the half-shadows. In fact, the artist has supplied so little information that there has even been some debate as to the subject of the painting, but the general consensus is that it shows the infant Moses holding Pharaoh's crown just prior to trampling on it as a symbolic rejection of Pharaoh's rule over the exiled Israelites. The elimination of all superfluous details allows the artist to concentrate on the psychological dimension of his subject. With an expression that combines the shock of recognition with consternation, Pharaoh appears already to acknowledge the true nature of the wilful child before him (see D.S. Pepper, 'A new late work by Guido Reni for Edinburgh and his late manner re-evaluated', *Burlington Magazine*, CXXI, 1979, pp.418–24).

Dozens of *abbozzi* of this kind are listed in Reni's post-mortem studio inventory and, as a picture executed in the last year or two of his life, one would expect to find mention of this canvas there. Accordingly, it has been tentatively suggested that its true subject eluded even the compilers of the inventory, and that it may be identical with a painting described as St Catherine (one of whose attributes is a crown) before the Emperor 'Massimino' [i.e. Maxentius], a subject not otherwise known to have been painted by Reni. According to the inventory, that picture had been ordered by Giulio Cesare Venenti, major-domo of the Cardinal Legate of Bologna, Giulio Sacchetti (see J.T. Spike, 'L' inventario dello studio di Guido Reni', *Accademia Clementina: Atti e Memorie*, 22, 1988, p.60). The picture's subject again went unrecognised in 1774, when it was described in the Bolognetti collection in Rome as a 'sketch of woman holding a child with a crown in his hand, presenting it to a man; Guido Reni'.

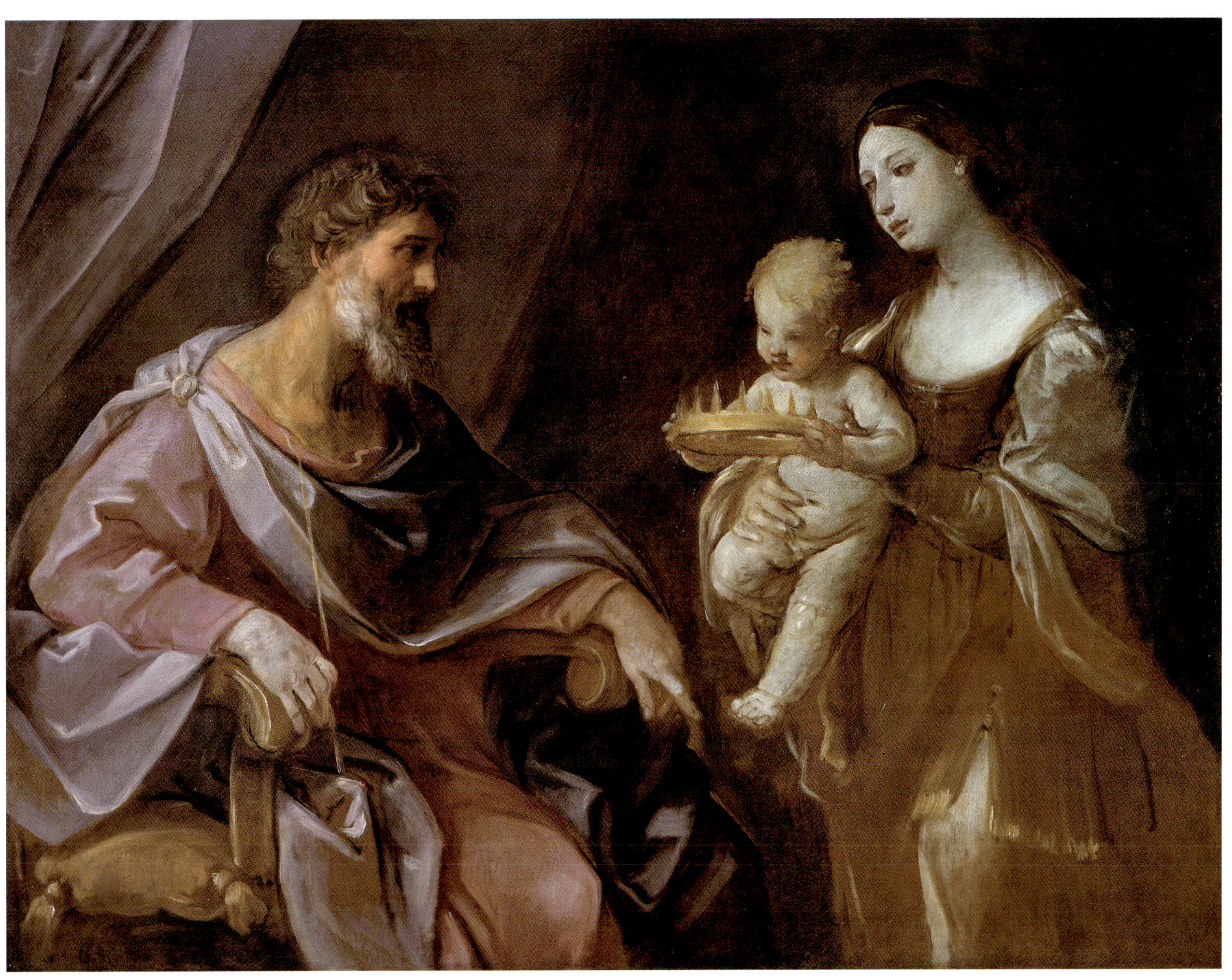

Giovanni Battista Gaulli, called Baciccio 1639–1709

9 *Portrait of Gianlorenzo Bernini, c.1675*

Oil on canvas · 39 × 29⅜in (99 × 74.5cm)
Purchased with the aid of the National Art Collections Fund 1998
NG 2694

This sympathetic and penetrating portrayal of the leading sculptor and architect of seventeenth-century Rome was painted around 1675, when Bernini (1598–1680) was in his late seventies. Clearly painted from life, its vibrant brushwork and bold touches of impasto mark it out as the prime version of a portrait known in numerous variants and copies. The sitter exudes an air of calm *gravitas*, and his obvious signs of ageing – wrinkled brow, hollowing cheeks and loose flaps of skin around the jowls – are offset by his alert gaze and the 'speaking gesture' of his hand emerging from the folds of his cloak. Although its complete provenance has not been established, this is almost certainly one of the five portraits of Bernini that appear, without attributions, in his post-mortem inventory and which were entailed to his descendants under the terms of his will (F. Borsi, C. Acidini Luchinat and F. Quinterio (eds.), *Gian Lorenzo Bernini: Il Testamento, la Casa, la Raccolta dei Beni*, Florence, 1981, pp.109, 118).

This appealing image of a brilliant but difficult man with a fiery temper and numerous detractors seems to have assumed the function of 'official' portrait of Bernini and to have been deliberately employed by his heirs to help foster a positive posthumous reputation. It served as the model for Arnold van Westerhout's engraved frontispiece to Filippo Baldinucci's flattering and polemical biography of Bernini, published in 1682, which, it has recently been shown, was largely 'ghosted' by Bernini's own son Pier Filippo (T. Montanari, 'Bernini e Cristina di Svezia: Alle origini della storiografia berniniana' in A. Angelini, *Gian Lorenzo Bernini e i Chigi tra Roma e Siena*, Siena, 1998, pp.401ff.). The Edinburgh painting was also the prototype for the portrait of Bernini commissioned later for the Roman Academy of St Luke. The best of the copies is a bust-length replica in a private collection, of which the head, at least, appears to be autograph (*Gian Lorenzo Bernini. Regista del Barocco*, exhibition catalogue, Palazzo Venezia, Rome, 1999, cat.no.15).

Baciccio was one of the foremost exponents of High Baroque decorative painting in Rome, best exemplified by his frescoes in the dome, pendentives, nave vault and apse of the Gesù, the Jesuit mother church (1672–85). However, it was evidently his talents as a portraitist that first established his reputation, although relatively few of these are known today (see F. Petrucci, 'La ritrattistica' in *Giovan Battista Gaulli, Il Baciccio 1639–1709*, exhibition catalogue, Palazzo Chigi, Ariccia, 1999–2000, pp.89–121). Genoese by birth and training, Baciccio moved to Rome around 1658. By the mid-1660s he was on close terms with Bernini, who did much to foster his career, and was instrumental in securing for him the important commission to decorate the pendentives of Sant'Agnese in Piazza Navona (1666–72), as well as the extensive Gesù frescoes mentioned above. It is especially fitting that Baciccio should, in turn, have been so directly involved in the perpetuation of his master's memory. Another portrait of Bernini by Baciccio, dating from about a decade earlier, is in the Galleria Nazionale d'Arte Antica at Palazzo Barberini, Rome (Rome, 1999, cat.no.14).

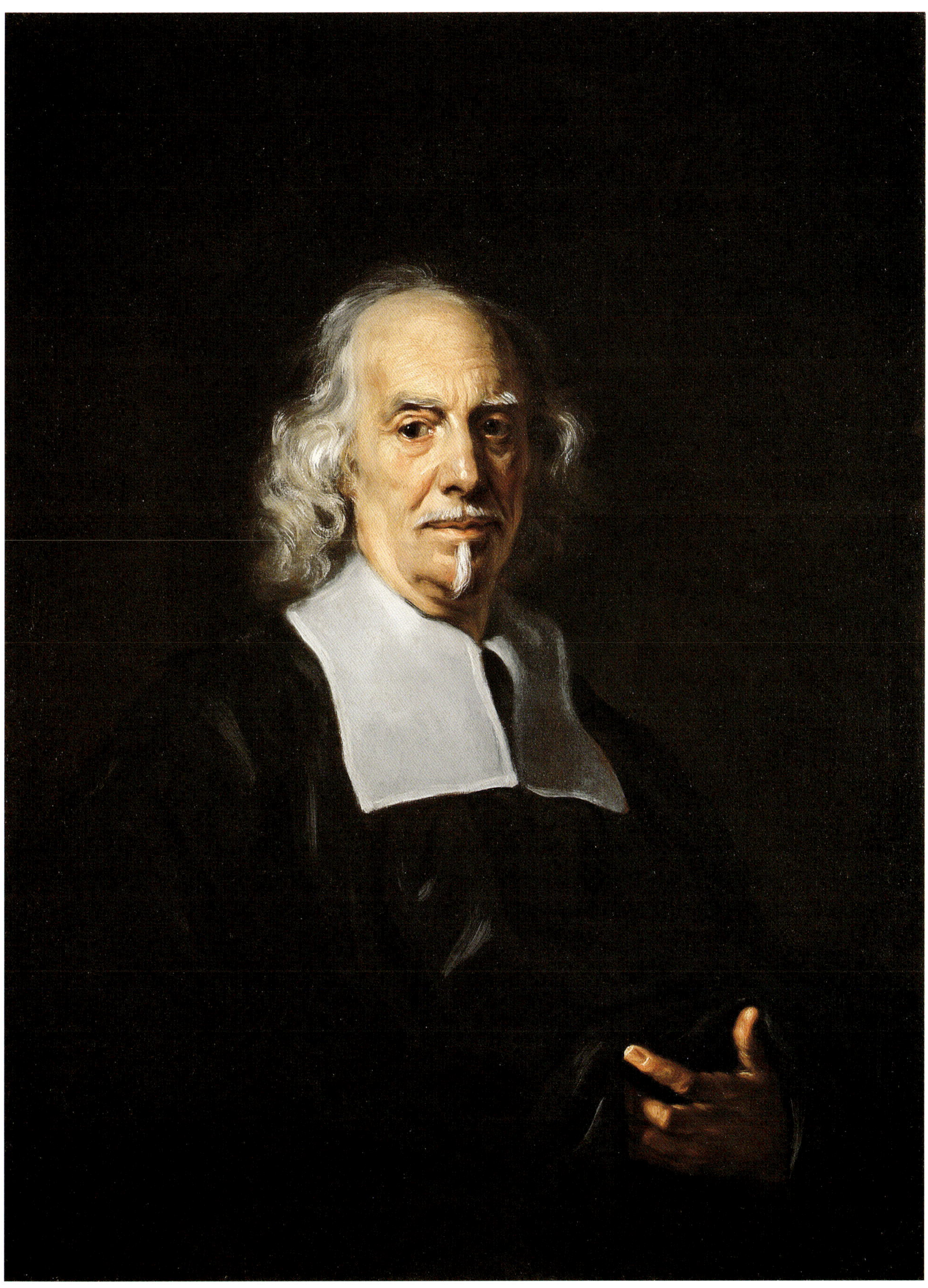

Antonio Canal, called Canaletto 1697–1768

10 *The Grand Canal, Venice, from the Campo San Vio, c.1725–30*

Oil on canvas · 26⅝ × 33¼in (67.6 × 84.5cm)
Purchased by the Royal Institution 1831; transferred to the National Gallery of Scotland 1858
NG 17

This view shows the Grand Canal looking east, as if the artist's vantage point were a window of the present-day Palazzo Cini. In the right foreground is the Campo San Vio, with a man relieving himself against the side elevation of the Palazzo Barbarigo. The perspective on this south side of the canal terminates in the Punta della Dogana (the old customs house) and includes, slightly set back, the majestic dome of Baldassare Longhena's masterpiece, Santa Maria della Salute. On the north side, the Palazzo Corner della Ca' Grande at the extreme left, built in the mid-sixteenth century to Jacopo Sansovino's design, is one of the grandest of all the palaces on the Grand Canal. Next to it, partly hidden, is the Palazzo Minotto, and beyond, in succession, the Palazzi Barbarigo, Manin Contarini, Venier Contarini and, projecting further into the canal, the Palazzi Pisani Gritti and Contarini Flangini Fini. In the distance, on the far side of the Bacino di San Marco, are the buildings fronting the Riva degli Schiavoni.

This was one of Canaletto's favourite Grand Canal views. At least twelve versions are known, each of which adopts a slightly different viewpoint and arrangement of boats and staffage (W. G. Constable, *Canaletto (1697–1768)*, second edition, revised by J. G. Links, 2 vols., Oxford, 1976, I, plates 39–41; II, pp.274–9, cat.nos.182–92). The first and largest of these (Museo Thyssen-Bornemisza, Madrid), dating from about 1720, is among the artist's earliest topographical views (*vedute*). He had previously assisted his father, who was a painter of theatrical scenery. By the mid-1720s Canaletto had surpassed Luca Carlevaris (1663/4–1730) – by whom he was much influenced – as the leading view painter in Venice. At about this time he was involved in a collaborative project for a series of *Allegorical Tombs* to British worthies commissioned by an Irish theatrical impresario, Owen McSwiney, and thereafter he worked almost exclusively for British patrons. Especially important was the relationship he established with Joseph Smith, later British Consul in Venice, who amassed a huge collection of Canaletto's work and acted as his intermediary with countless other British clients. The artist was himself resident in England for most of the period 1746–55.

Although the Edinburgh painting entered the collection as a Canaletto, it was subsequently demoted and catalogued as the work of a follower. However, recent cleaning (1995) has revealed its high quality, and it has again been accepted as an autograph work, dating from the second half of the 1720s. Several of the other versions of this composition date from the same period, including one from the collection of Joseph Smith (now Royal Collection, Windsor Castle) which was engraved by Antonio Visentini and published in the *Prospectus Magni Canalis Venetiarum* (1735), a series of fourteen views after Canaletto's paintings of the Grand Canal. Stylistically, the Edinburgh painting is particularly close to the larger versions in the Brooks Memorial Art Gallery, Memphis (Constable-Links, 1976, I, pl.40; II, p.276, cat.no.187) and in a private collection (J. G. Links, *A Supplement to W.G. Constable's 'Canaletto'*, London, 1998, p.19, cat.no.186, pl.255).

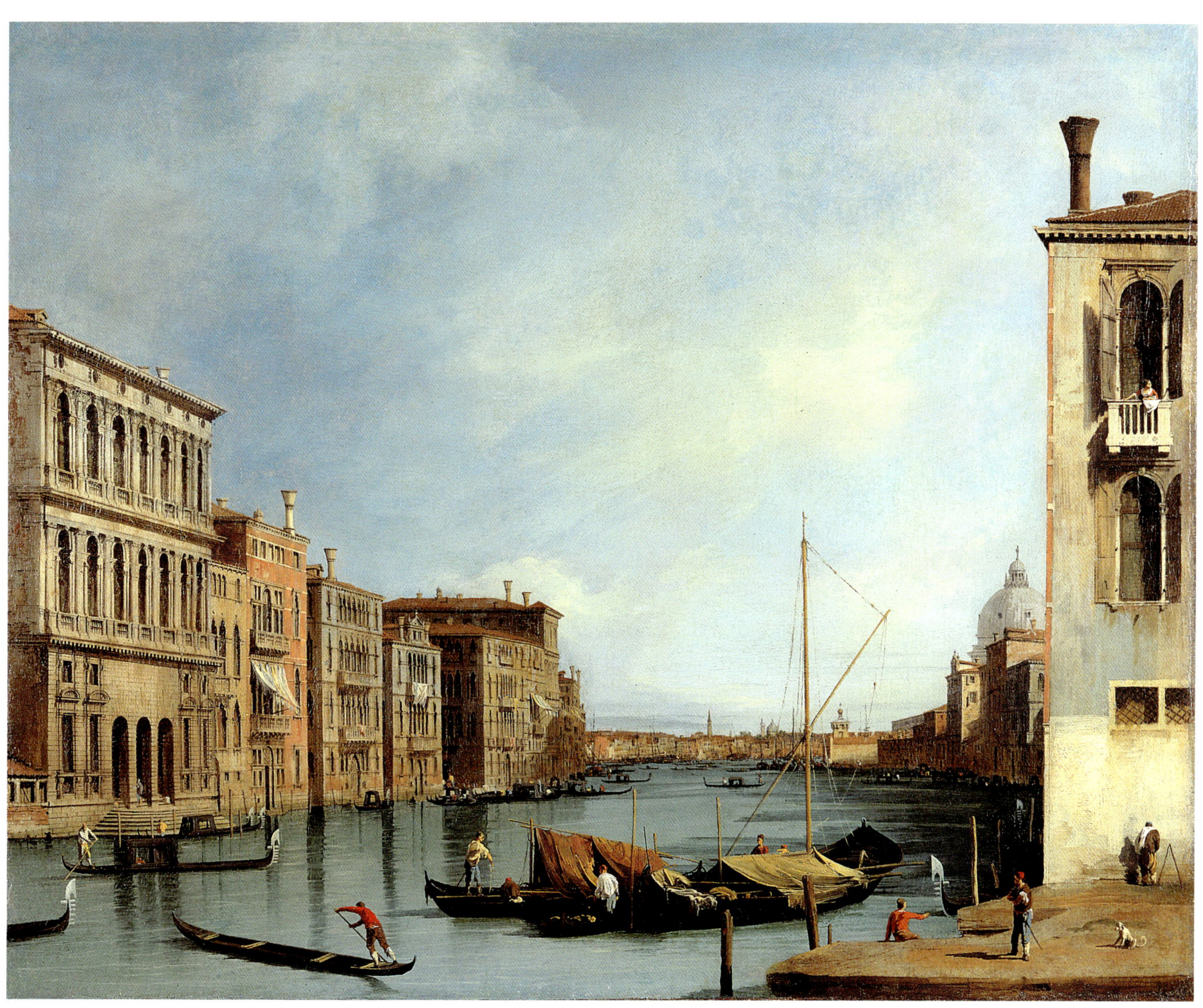

Pompeo Batoni 1708–1787

11 *Portrait of Alexander, 4th Duke of Gordon*, 1764

Oil on canvas · 115 × 75½in (292 × 192cm)
Signed and dated at the lower right: P. BATONI PINXIT ROMÆ. 1764.
Purchased by Private Treaty from the Trustees of the Goodwood Collection with the aid of the National Heritage Memorial Fund and the National Art Collections Fund 1994
NG 2589

Although rightly best known for his outstanding talents as a portraitist, Batoni's early success was as a history painter. The demand for portraits from his hand rocketed around 1750 and thereafter it became virtually de rigueur for distinguished visitors to Rome, especially British and Irish aristocrats on the Grand Tour, to sit to Batoni.

The 4th Duke of Gordon (1743–1827) succeeded to the title in 1752 while still a boy. On leaving Eton he received a captain's commission in the 89th Regiment of Foot, and was made Colonel in 1763. The regiment, known as the Gordon Highlanders, had been raised on the duke's estates for the service of the government by his step-father, General Morris. Gordon did the Grand Tour in 1762–3, arriving in Rome in December 1762, and remaining there at least until March. He must have sat to Batoni on this visit, although the resulting portrait was not completed until the following year. Gordon served for much of his life as a representative peer for Scotland and held numerous public offices, including Keeper of the Great Seal of Scotland and Lord Lieutenant of Aberdeenshire. He was created a Knight of the Thistle in 1775, and Earl of Norwich in 1784. In his youth he was reputed to be the most handsome man in Scotland. He married his first wife, the beautiful and unconventional Jane Maxwell, in 1767, and although they had six children, they were later bitterly estranged. She died in 1812, and eight years later the duke married his mistress, Jane Christie, with whom he had already had a large illegitimate family.

In this portrait, the attributes of learning and references to classical antiquity that flatter most of Batoni's sitters are absent, and Gordon's passion for field sports and rural pursuits is emphasised instead. He is shown standing elegantly beside his mount, the epitome of aristocratic poise and confidence, with his prized hounds and the spoils of the day's hunt at his feet, and an evocation of Gordon Castle in the distance. The duke was evidently far from overwhelmed by the grandeur of the Eternal City: having had the good sense to engage Johann Joachim Winckelmann, the German theorist and champion of Neoclassicism, as his guide, he 'showed scarcely a trace of animation as he sat in his carriage, while Winckelmann described to him, with the choicest expressions and grandest illustrations, the beauties of the ancient works of art' (J. Ingamells, *A Dictionary of British and Irish Travellers in Italy 1701–1800, compiled from the Brinsley Ford Archive*, New Haven and London, 1997, p.408).

Batoni nevertheless based Gordon's pose loosely on that of a celebrated antique statue, the *Apollo Belvedere* (A.M. Clark, *Pompeo Batoni: Complete Catalogue*, edited by E.P. Bowron, Oxford, 1985, p.297, cat.no.279).

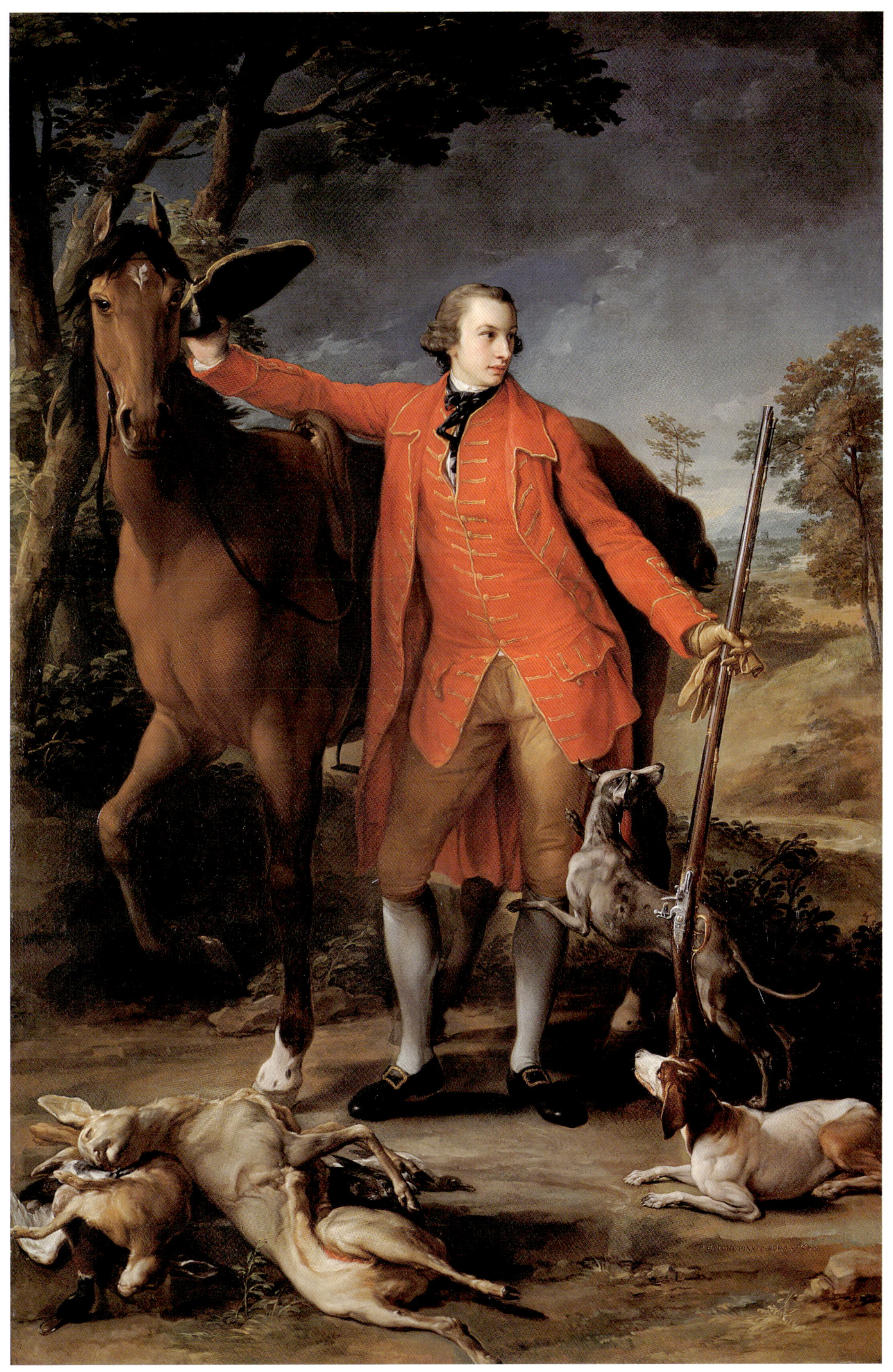

Francesco Guardi 1712–1793

12 *The Piazza San Marco, Venice, c.* 1775–80

Oil on canvas · 21¾ × 33⅝in (55.2 × 85.4cm)
Accepted in lieu of tax from the Estate of the 14th Duke of Hamilton and allocated to the National Gallery of Scotland 1978
NG 2370

Guardi is the most famous Venetian view painter of the eighteenth century after Canaletto, by whom he was influenced. He appears to have turned his attention to topographical views (*vedute*) only in the 1750s, although there are few fixed points of reference to help in establishing his chronology. A recently discovered painting of *The Mardí Gras Festival in the Piazzetta* is dated 1756 (private collection, London), and Guardi is documented as having exhibited two topographical views in 1764. He had been active during the 1730s and 1740s as a figure painter, often in collaboration with his talented older brother Gian Antonio, who was probably his teacher. Francesco was certainly more accomplished as a landscapist than as a history painter, and the shift in his production enabled him to exploit the lucrative market for *vedute* established by Canaletto. Compared to the crystalline clarity and precision of the latter's mature works, Guardi's views of Venice are characterised by a more rapid and impressionistic touch, and a greater feeling for more transient effects of light and atmosphere. Like Canaletto, he certainly made use of a camera obscura for his topographical views, and he sometimes based his compositions on engravings after other artists, including Canaletto.

The Piazza San Marco, the hub of Venetian civic and religious life, was painted repeatedly by Guardi from various angles. The main market for these paintings lay with foreign tourists eager for a momento of this spectacular urban space. The Edinburgh painting, which probably dates from about 1775–80 (A. Morassi, *Guardi: I dipinti*, 2 vols., Milan, 1984, I, p.372, cat.no.327), shows the principal view of the square looking towards the façade of the Basilica of San Marco, its mosaics shimmering in the sunlight. Behind the *campanile* (bell-tower) is a glimpse of the Doge's Palace, while at the sides the view is framed by the receding arcades of the Procuratie Vecchie and Nuove, the former casting a strong shadow over much of the piazza. The scene is enlivened by traders, uniformed government officials and fashionably dressed tourists and promenaders, all sketched in with a few deft strokes of the brush. Guardi depicts the *campanile* as slightly taller and slenderer than it is in reality, a peculiarity he seems to have adopted from Canaletto. A painting in the National Gallery, London, generally dated to about 1760, is probably the earliest of Guardi's numerous versions of this composition (see *Francesco Guardi: Vedute, Capricci, Feste*, exhibition catalogue, Fondazione Giorgio Cini, Venice, 1993, pp.102–3, cat.no.28).

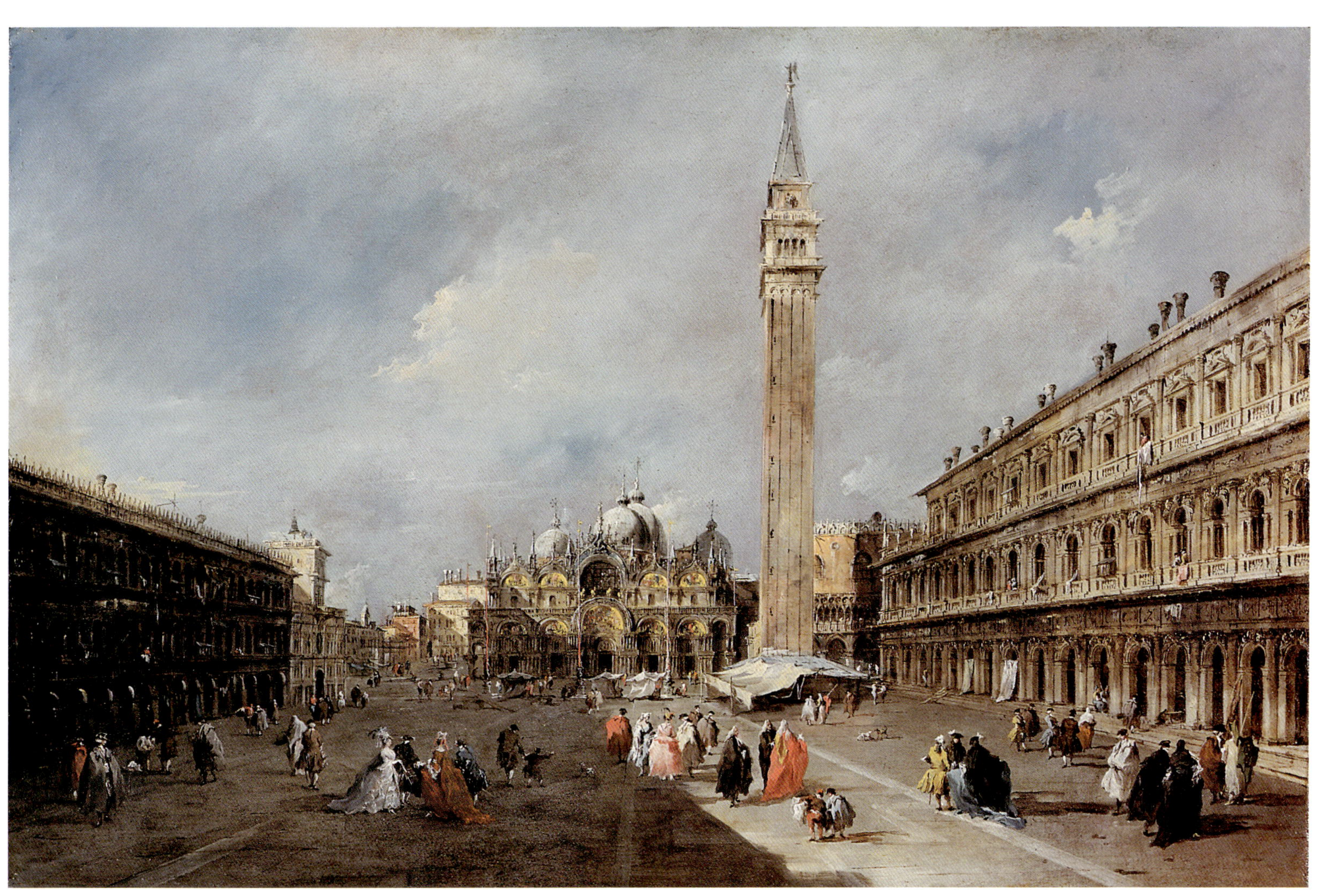

El Greco 1541–1614

13 *Christ Blessing ('The Saviour of the World')*, *c.*1600

Oil on canvas · 28¾ × 22¼in (73 × 56.5cm)
Signed at the centre right in cursive Greek initials: δ. φ.
Purchased 1952
NG 2160

His real name was Domenikos Theotokopoulos, but he is universally known by his Spanish sobriquet El Greco ('the Greek'). He was trained in the Byzantine tradition of his native Crete, but his style transformed after he moved to Venice, where he is recorded in 1568 and where he was reportedly a pupil of Titian. He was in Rome in the service of the Farnese family by 1570, and in 1577 he settled permanently in Toledo in Spain. Within a few years he had perfected his highly idiosyncratic mature style which remained essentially unchanged until his death. As a result, the dating of his undocumented pictures, including the present one, is often rather approximate. The output of his Toledo workshop was prodigious, with many compositions surviving in multiple versions.

The pale, gaunt *Saviour of the World* (*Salvator Mundi*) is here shown with his right hand raised in the Latin gesture of benediction, and with the spidery fingers of his left hand resting on the crystalline orb of the world. The direct, frontal presentation of Christ recalls the hieratic Byzantine tradition of El Greco's youth, although in the Eastern Church he would normally have been shown as 'Pantocrator', with a gospel-book rather than a globe (see *El Greco: Mystery and Illumination*, exhibition catalogue, National Gallery of Scotland, Edinburgh, 1989, p.71, cat.no.22). Immediate precedents for the imagery adopted here can be found in the work of Titian, notably his painting of *c.*1570 in the State Hermitage Museum, St Petersburg (H.E. Wethey, *Titian: The Religious Paintings*, London, 1969, pp.77–8, cat.no.18). The Edinburgh canvas was evidently painted quickly, using loose, expressive brushstrokes over a warm reddish-brown ground, which is left visible in parts of the globe and the background. The globe reflects the pale ice blue of Christ's mantle, which is set off against the warm crimson of his robe, a contrast typical of El Greco's palette. The flickering, ethereal illumination was achieved by using unmixed white for the highlights, a practice that has its ultimate origins in his earliest Cretan works. The painting is usually dated to around 1600 or slightly earlier.

This is one of the finest of several closely related versions of this composition by El Greco and his workshop (see H.E. Wethey, *El Greco and his School*, 2 vols., Princeton, 1962, II, pp.71–2; 99–108). At least three of these belong to series of canvases representing Christ and the twelve apostles, which are known in Spain as *Apostolados*, and there is every possibility that the Edinburgh painting did too. Two complete three-quarter-length series of this kind by El Greco survive, one of about 1600 or shortly afterwards in the sacristy of Toledo Cathedral, the other, dating from the very end of the artist's life (*c.*1608–14), in the Museo del Greco, Toledo. A half-length series of the twelve apostles alone, but missing the figure of Christ, is in the collection of the Marqués de San Feliz, and other half-length series are now dispersed. El Greco's earliest surviving representation of this subject is a painting dating from the 1580s in a private collection (*Six Centuries of Old Master Paintings*, exhibition catalogue, Harari & Johns Ltd, London, 1989, cat.no.31). Two entries in the artist's post-mortem inventory seem to confirm that he occasionally treated the *Salvator Mundi* as an independent subject.

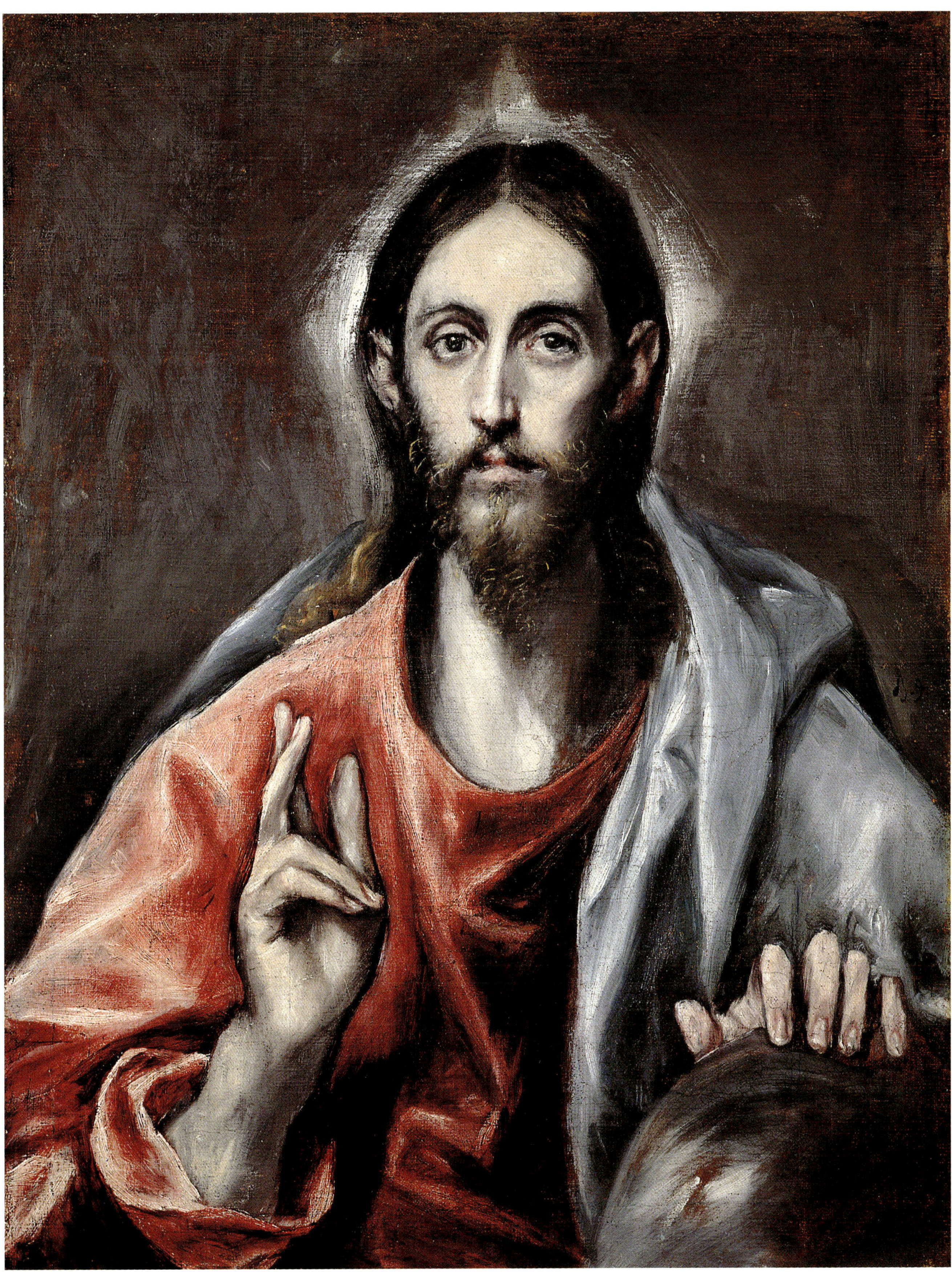

Francisco de Goya 1746–1828

14 *El médico (The Doctor)*, 1779

Oil on canvas · 37¾ × 47⅜in (95.8 × 120.2cm) (cut down)
Purchased 1923
NG 1628

Equally accomplished as a painter and printmaker, Goya was one of the most original and enigmatic artists of his age. He managed to combine a highly successful public career dominated by portraiture with the creation of the more personal and imaginative works, often with violent or fantastic subject matter, for which he is now most famous. Goya was from the province of Zaragoza in north-eastern Spain, and was apprenticed in 1760 for four years to the local painter José Luzan, although by 1763 he was already studying under Francisco Bayeu in Madrid. In 1770–1 he was in Italy. He settled in Madrid in 1774 and began work on the first of several series of designs for the Royal Tapestry Works. In 1780 Goya became a member of the Madrid Academy. He was appointed *pintor del rey* (painter to the king) in 1786 and was promoted to the top position, *primer pintor de cámara* (first painter to the court), in 1799. A serious illness in 1793 left him permanently deaf. He remained in Madrid during the French occupation (1808–13) and again worked for the Spanish monarchy after its restoration. He spent the last years of his life in voluntary exile in Bordeaux in France.

El médico is one of a group of eleven tapestry cartoons that Goya delivered to the Royal Tapestry Factory in January 1780 (for full details see *Goya, 250 Aniversario*, exhibition catalogue, Museo del Prado, Madrid, 1996, pp.305–14, cat.nos.25–34). Since the previous batch of cartoons was delivered in July 1779, *El médico* was almost certainly painted in the latter part of that year. The related tapestry formed part of a series of thirteen that decorated the antechamber of the Princes of Asturias in the Royal Palace of El Pardo in Madrid. Goya had already provided tapestry designs for the dining room and the bedroom in these apartments. The three series illustrated the broad theme of the diversions, customs and fashions of the time, a programme that seems to have allowed the artist a considerable measure of creative freedom.

From a document of October 1777, we know that the final tapestry of *El médico* was to be hung above a door on one of the short walls of the antechamber, and Goya took account of this high location: the viewpoint is low, the design relatively simple, the colours bold, and the few bulky figures silhouetted clearly against the sky. Goya's invoice for the painting describes the subject as 'A doctor seated, warming himself at a brazier; some books on the ground by his side, behind him two students'. Quite how this relates to the overall theme of the room is unclear. It has been noted that a man warming his hands and a leafless tree are both emblems of Winter, but none of the other subjects in the series explicitly relates to the seasons. The tapestry of *El médico* was paired on the opposite wall with *La cita* (*The Rendezvous*), the cartoon for which is in the Prado (Madrid, 1996, cat.no.33). Dominated by the reclining figure of a woman in contemporary dress in a pose traditionally associated with melancholy, its meaning in the context of the room is equally enigmatic. The Edinburgh canvas would originally have been about the same size as *La cita* (100 × 151 cm), but was cut down at an unknown date, conceivably around the time of its theft from the Palacio Real in Madrid during the revolution of 1868–9.

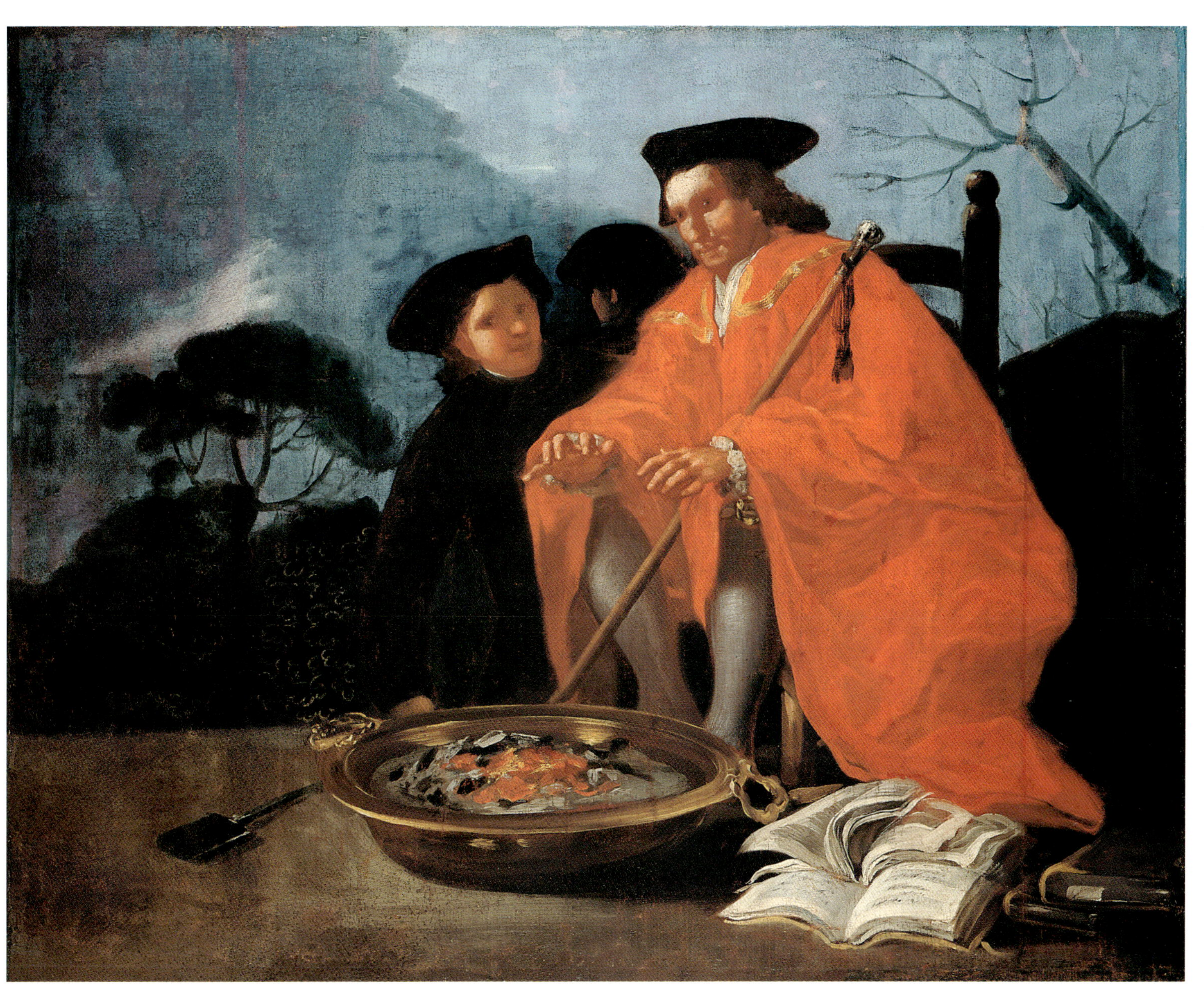

Paulus Moreelse 1571–1638

15 *A Shepherd with a Pipe*, *c*.1625–30

Oil on canvas · 37¼ × 28⅝in (94.8 × 72.7cm)
Purchased by the Royal Institution 1831; transferred to the National Gallery of Scotland 1859
NG 52

Paulus Moreelse was born in Utrecht, a lively centre for painting in the Netherlands. Unusually for the predominantly Protestant and middle-class cities of the United Provinces, Utrecht retained a bias towards Catholicism and nobility. This prompted a certain cosmopolitan taste amongst Utrecht citizens, provided for by artists whose work had an international character, inspired by their travels in Italy, or elsewhere abroad.

Moreelse trained with the Delft portrait painter Michiel van Mierevelt, but travelled to Italy where he stayed for some years, returning to Utrecht by 1596. He became a key figure in Utrecht, a founder of the painters' guild in 1611, and a master at the Drawing Academy where he taught with Abraham Bloemaert, with no less than twenty-eight pupils recorded. Moreelse also played his part in civic duties as a city councillor, treasurer and alderman. His work gained popularity both locally and across the country and his clients included the Duke of Braunschweig and other notables.

This half-length of a shepherd represents a type of pastoral composition which Moreelse played a crucial role in popularising in the Netherlands, presumably influenced by his Italian sojourn (see A. McNeil Kettering, *The Dutch Arcadia. Pastoral Art and Its Audience in the Golden Age*, Totawa and Montclair, New Jersey, 1983, pp.34–5, fig.5). The herder with his simple shirt, rough fleece around him, and a flower and stalk of corn placed jauntily in his feathered cap, symbolised the untrammelled existence of a shepherd in a mythical Arcadia: free of care to live and love as the summer day is long. The theme originates from classical literature such as Virgil's *Eclogues* and *Georgics,* poems celebrating 'the simple life' of farmers and shepherds, which were popular in the Netherlands and were translated by the artist and critic Karel van Mander in 1597. Contemporary Italian and Dutch writing also warmed to this subject, most particularly in Giovanni Battista Guarini's play of 1589, *Il Pastor Fido* (*The Faithful Shepherd*) and Pieter Cornelisz. Hooft's tribute to Guarini, first performed in 1605, *Granida en Daifilo,* where Princess Granida falls in love with Daifilo, a shepherd.

Emulated in popular pastoral poems and love songs, the subject also became fashionable in Dutch art. One of the earliest known examples appears to have been a half-length *Shepherdess* by Moreelse of 1617 (private collection), who also painted *A Shepherd* and *Shepherdess* as pendant works in 1622 (Krayer-La Roche Collection, Basel). Such gentle erudition and light-hearted amorous content appealed to the court at The Hague, and similar works were owned by Prince Frederick Hendrick and Amalia van Solms. It is likely that the Edinburgh picture, probably painted in the mid- to late 1620s, represents the poet Virgil's faithful shepherd Coridon, who is taught to play his pipe by Venus' son Cupid. There may also have been a pendant to the Edinburgh canvas, presumably of Coridon's love, Sylvia. These pastoral figures were also used as the basis for portraits of the fashionable, though it is perhaps unlikely that the Edinburgh picture was intended as such a *portrait historié* (historical portrait).

In the light of Moreelse's Italian trip and the ultimately Italian nature of the subject of this work, it is noteworthy that the painting was in the Gerini collection in Florence by 1786 when it was engraved in a catalogue of eighty paintings from the collection (attributed to 'Morinello') and later appeared in the sale of the Marchese Giovanni Gerini which took place on 1 December 1825 as by 'Morillo' (lot 278).

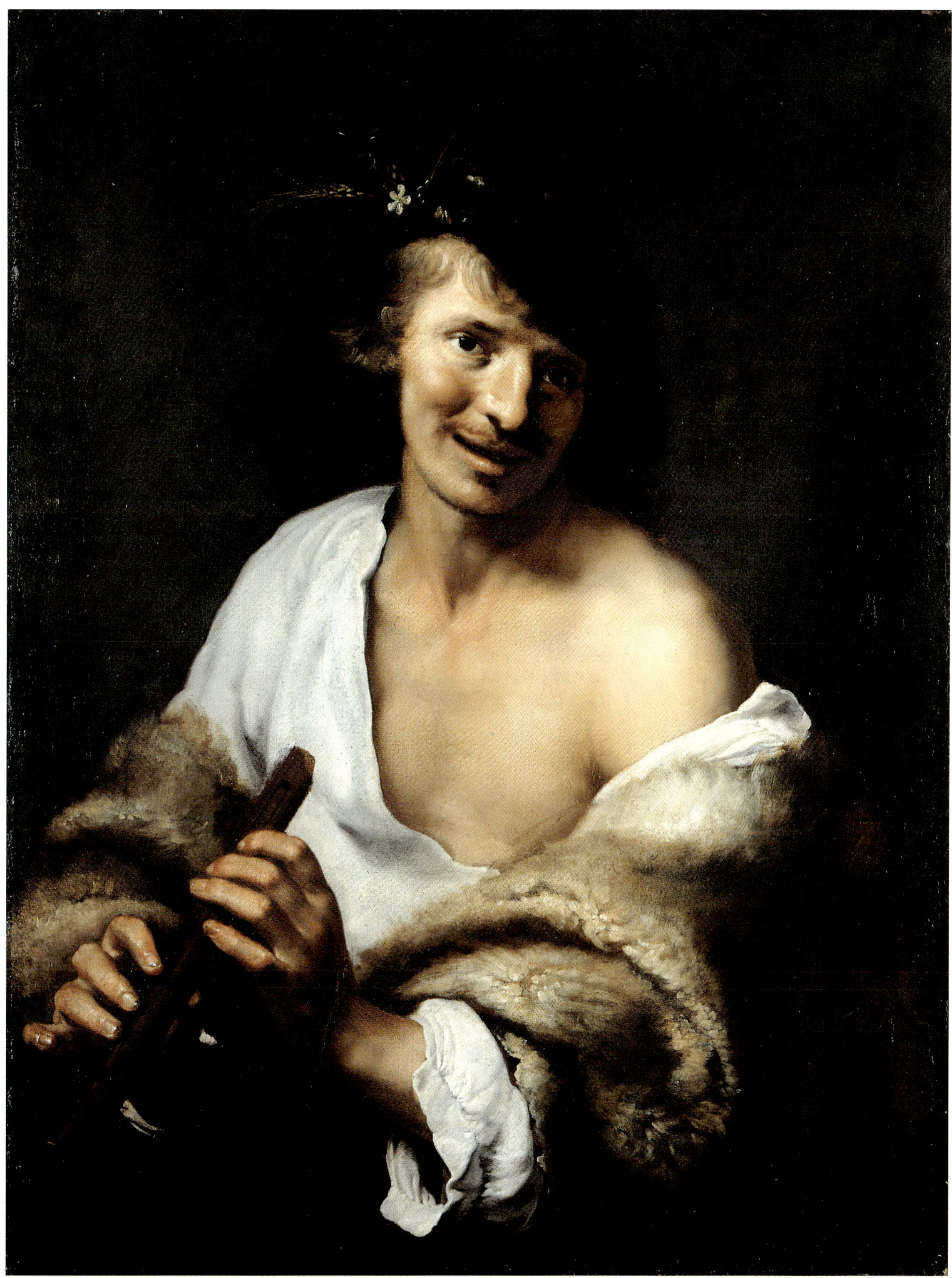

Frans Snyders 1579–1657

16 *Mischievous Monkeys, c.1630s*

Oil on canvas · 38⅛ × 45¼in (96.8 × 115cm)
Purchased by the Royal Institution for the National Gallery of Scotland 1867
NG 532

Frans Snyders was an extremely successful artist who specialised in painting animals and still life for which he displayed extraordinary talent and facility. He often worked independently, as in this picture of *Mischievous Monkeys*, but his skills were also greatly sought after by many other artists in Antwerp who employed him to complete parts of their pictures in which he excelled: flowers, fruit, feathers and fur. Such collaborations were not uncommon in seventeenth-century Flanders and Snyders joined forces with, most famously, Peter Paul Rubens, Anthony van Dyck and Jacob Jordaens. He is also documented as having worked with at least six other artists connected with Rubens's studio at various times: Erasmus Quellinus, Jan Wildens, Theodoor van Thulden, Cornelis de Vos, Jan Boeckhorst and Thomas Willeboirts Bosschaert. It is interesting, however, that in a painting by Willem van Haecht (1593–1637) portraying the prestigious visit of the Regents of the Spanish Netherlands to the celebrated *Art Collection of Cornelis van der Geest* (Rubenshuis, Antwerp) showing assembled works by Antwerp's elite artists, the picture by which Snyders is represented, propped up prominently by a table in the foreground, is a composition of monkeys and fruit similar to the Edinburgh canvas, painted by Snyders alone.

Snyders was born in Antwerp where he trained in the busy workshop of Pieter Brueghel the Younger. He became friends with his master's brother, the artist Jan Brueghel, who wrote to recommend the young Frans to his former patron, Cardinal Federigo Borromeo, in Milan when Frans travelled to Italy in 1608. Following his Italian visit, Snyders settled in Antwerp and married Margaretha, the sister of the painters Cornelis and Paul de Vos, in 1611. It is perhaps hardly surprising that Snyders collaborated with so many artists in the bustling artistic centre that Antwerp had become, given his own connections. Shortly before his marriage, he started working with Rubens (notably painting the eagle in Rubens's *Prometheus Bound*, Philadelphia Museum of Art) and continued to participate in Rubens's workshop for the next thirty years.

There was a strong tradition of excellence in still-life painting in Antwerp but Snyders conceived such subject-matter in a far grander manner than his predecessors. His dramatic and elaborate scenes are exquisitely painted. Through use of bright colours, dynamic patterns and sumptuous textures, Snyders produced compositions full of vitality. In this painting *Mischievous Monkeys*, probably dating from about the 1630s, the destructive monkeys (less sinister than those that feature in the work of Jan Brueghel or David Teniers) are beautifully observed in the extravagant havoc that they wreak. Snyders re-used elements of this composition in a number of his other works and incorporated this motif of the same table with fruit and monkeys in a larger painting now in the Prado Museum, Madrid. Given the larger format of the Prado work, the question poses itself as to whether the Edinburgh canvas was also once part of a bigger composition. During conservation in 1989, it was noticed that the tacking edges of the canvas only survive on the left, so the other three sides may have been trimmed, although to what extent it is not possible to tell. However, a drawing by Snyders recording a very similar composition (Christie's, Amsterdam, 13 November 1995, lot.71, repr.) shows that this rather oddly clipped format, also with a similarly 'curtailed' half monkey at the right, was part of Snyders's artistic repertoire. The Edinburgh canvas may, therefore, not have actually been very much bigger, though the composition perhaps extended at the right to include the whole of the glass vase of tulips.

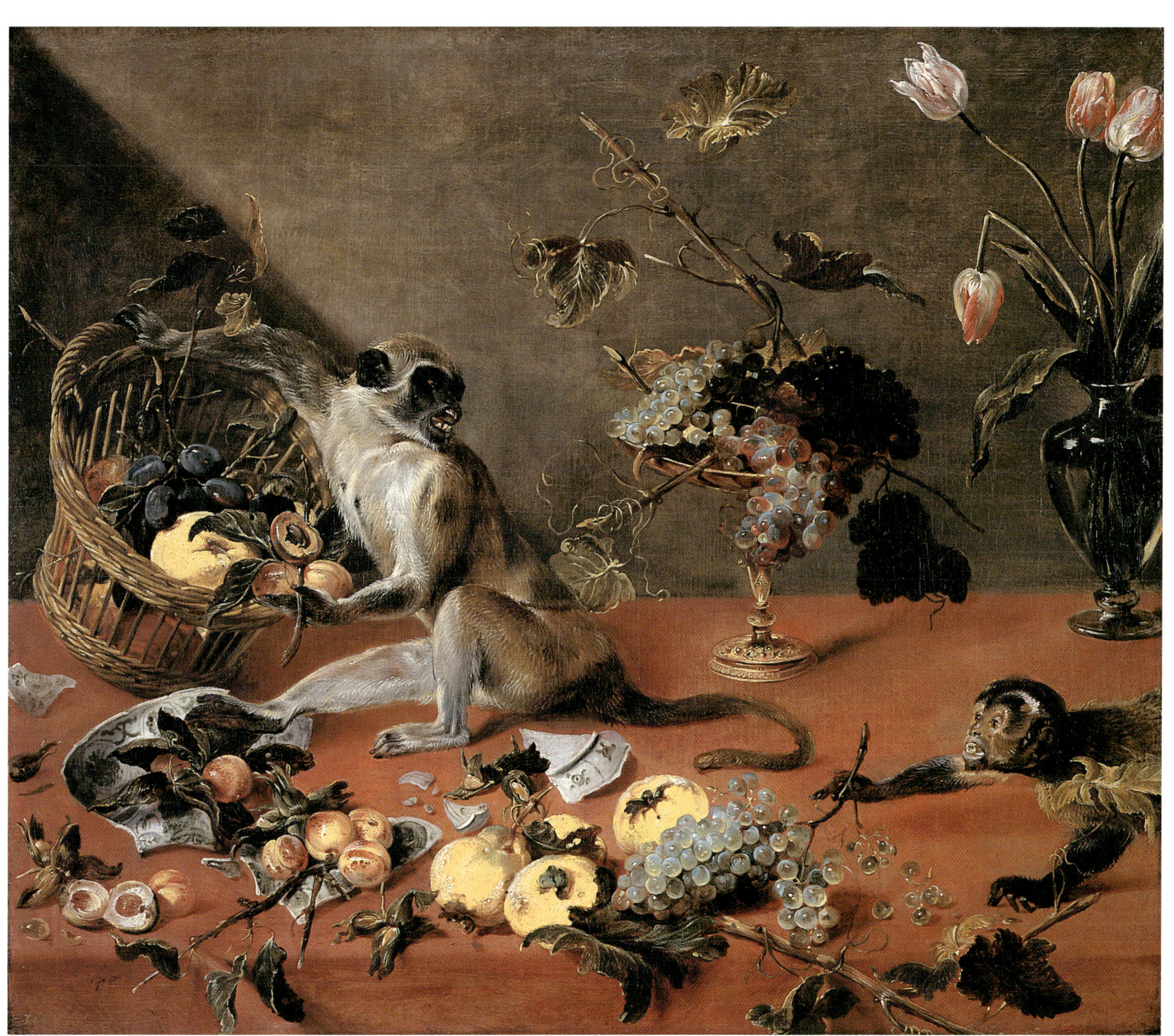

Frans Hals *c.*1580/85–1666

17 *A Dutch Gentleman*, *c.*1643–5

Oil on canvas · 45¼ × 33⅞in (115 × 86.1cm)
Presented by the Rt Hon. William McEwan 1885
NG 691

This portrait, a pendant to that of *A Dutch Lady* (see no.18), was probably painted between 1643 and 1645, a date indicated by the style of the work and a likely dating for the clothes the couple wear (see S. Slive, *Frans Hals*, London, 1974, III, p.80, cat.nos.156–7). Before about 1640 Hals often included a chair next to his patrons when shown standing, but he subsequently eliminated this motif from his pendant portraits to focus more completely upon the figures themselves, as we see here.

Hals was the unrivalled master of portraiture in Haarlem in the seventeenth century. He is famous for his accomplished and animated likenesses of the city's regent class, militia and wealthy merchants, but he also painted a number of genre scenes and some religious works. He was probably born in Antwerp but his family left sometime after the city's fall to the Spanish in August 1585 and fled north to the United Provinces. The family had settled in Haarlem by 1591 where Hals spent most of his life. The artist and writer Karel van Mander (1548–1606) stated that Hals trained with him before 1603, although no obvious influence of Van Mander's practice or, indeed, theory is noticeable in his pupil's work. Van Mander certainly did not rate the status of a portrait painter highly, in his view an occupation that brought neither glory nor gold.

Hals entered the Haarlem painters' guild as an independent artist in 1610. He visited Antwerp (where he probably saw works by Rubens) in 1616, the year that saw the start of his unresolved financial problems. Hals's talent was not unrecognised by his patrons, indeed he had been praised as early as 1628 by Samuel Ampzing for his ability to capture the spirit of his sitters, and he received a number of important commissions including religious, civic and militia and banquet groups. However, despite this, he seems to have been permanently in debt, even when his business was thriving in the 1630s. In addition, his first wife had died young, leaving two small children, and his marriage to Lysbeth Regnier proceeded to provide yet eight more progeny (one baptised nine days after the wedding). She was cautioned several times by the civic magistrates for affray while he was continually served with demands for repayment. It was only in 1662 that he received a small annuity from the Haarlem council to ease his financial circumstances.

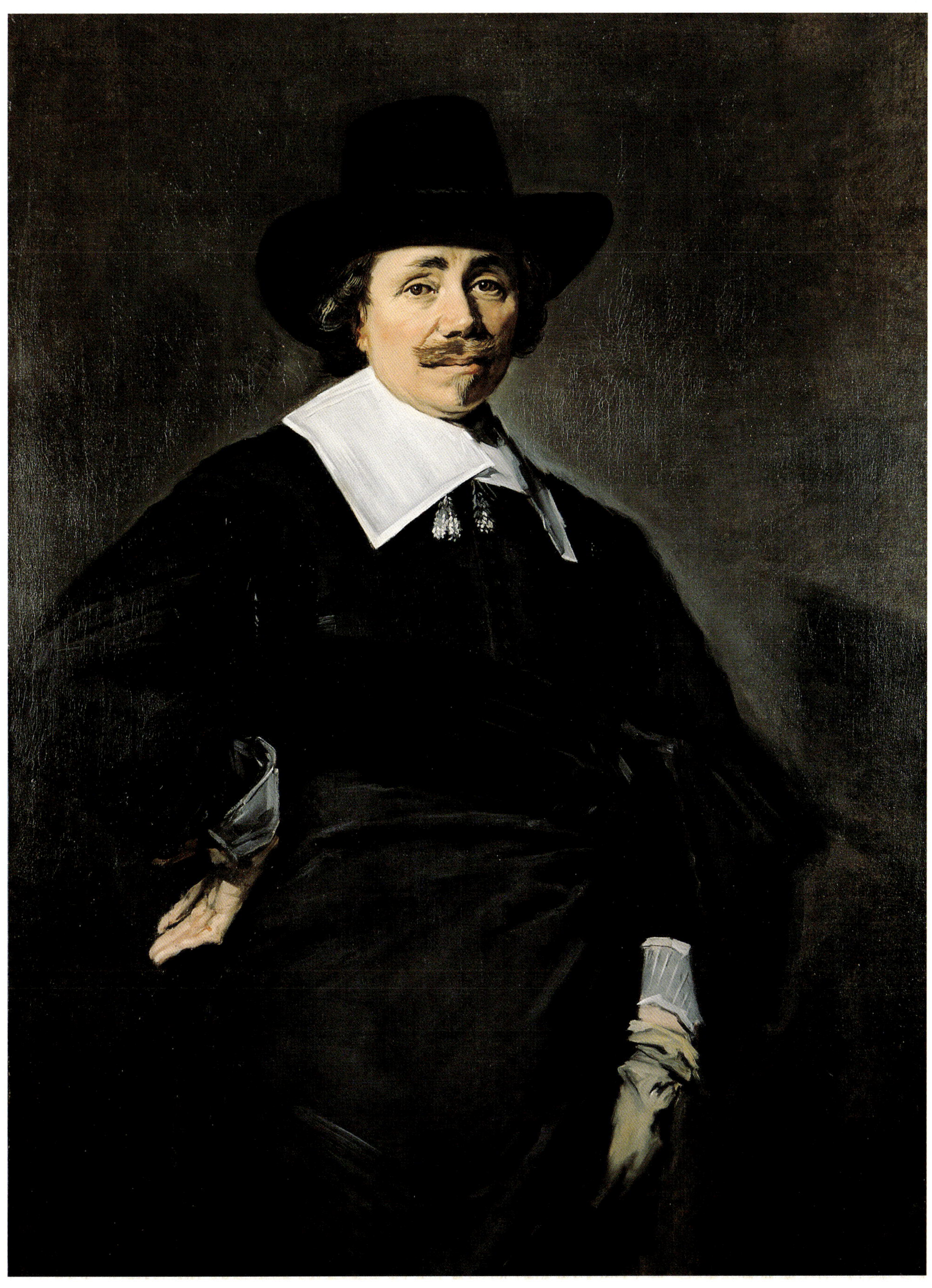

Frans Hals *c.*1580/85–1666

18 *A Dutch Lady*, *c.*1643–5

Oil on canvas · 45¼ × 33¾in (115 × 85.8cm)
Presented by the Rt Hon. William McEwan 1885
NG 692

This portrait and no.17, painted between about 1643 and 1645, show wealthy though as yet unidentified sitters. Hals's portraiture became rather smoother in manner between the 1630s and 1640s, employing predominantly black costumes and more static poses. However, despite his tonal restraint in certain areas of the compositions, this only serves to accentuate the brilliance of other passages, such as the masterful painting of the woman's neckerchief, justifiably called by the Hals scholar Seymour Slive 'a dazzling display of Hals's wizardry with white'. This would have been the latest style in fashion by 1645, for these large cambric cloths folded in various ways had begun to replace the now outdated circular millstone ruffs. Her cap (*tipmuts*) and loose hair also aid dating the painting since before about 1640 fashion dictated that hair was put up and covered with a cap.

Hals is documented as having only two pupils, his son-in-law, Pieter Gerritz. van Roestraeten (1627–1698) and Vincent Laurensz. van Vinne (1628–1702), but there were likely a number more and his style also influenced the more famous artist Judith Leyster and her husband Jan Miense Molenaer. Despite the high reputation he earned during his lifetime, Hals's work fell rapidly out of favour after his death. Enthusiasm for his talent was only rekindled in the late nineteenth century, perhaps due to a new appreciation of his broad brushstrokes and 'wet-on-wet' bravura of handling (formerly seen as slapdash) as a type of proto-Impressionism. Van Gogh admired him 'as a colourist amongst colourists', remarking that Hals had at least 'twenty-seven different shades of black'.

William McEwan, MP for Edinburgh, and wealthy brewer of McEwan's ale at Fountainbridge in Edinburgh, was keenly interested in Dutch painting, attested by his own collection, much of which can now be seen at Polesden Lacey, owned by the National Trust. Partly because of his own enthusiasm and his position as MP for Edinburgh, McEwan decided the National Gallery of Scotland should be able to represent two of what he presumably perceived to be the finest Dutch painters and he purchased these two portraits by Hals and later put up the money for the purchase of Rembrandt's *A Woman in Bed* for the Gallery. The two Hals portraits had previously belonged to a Major Jackson of St Andrews in Fife.

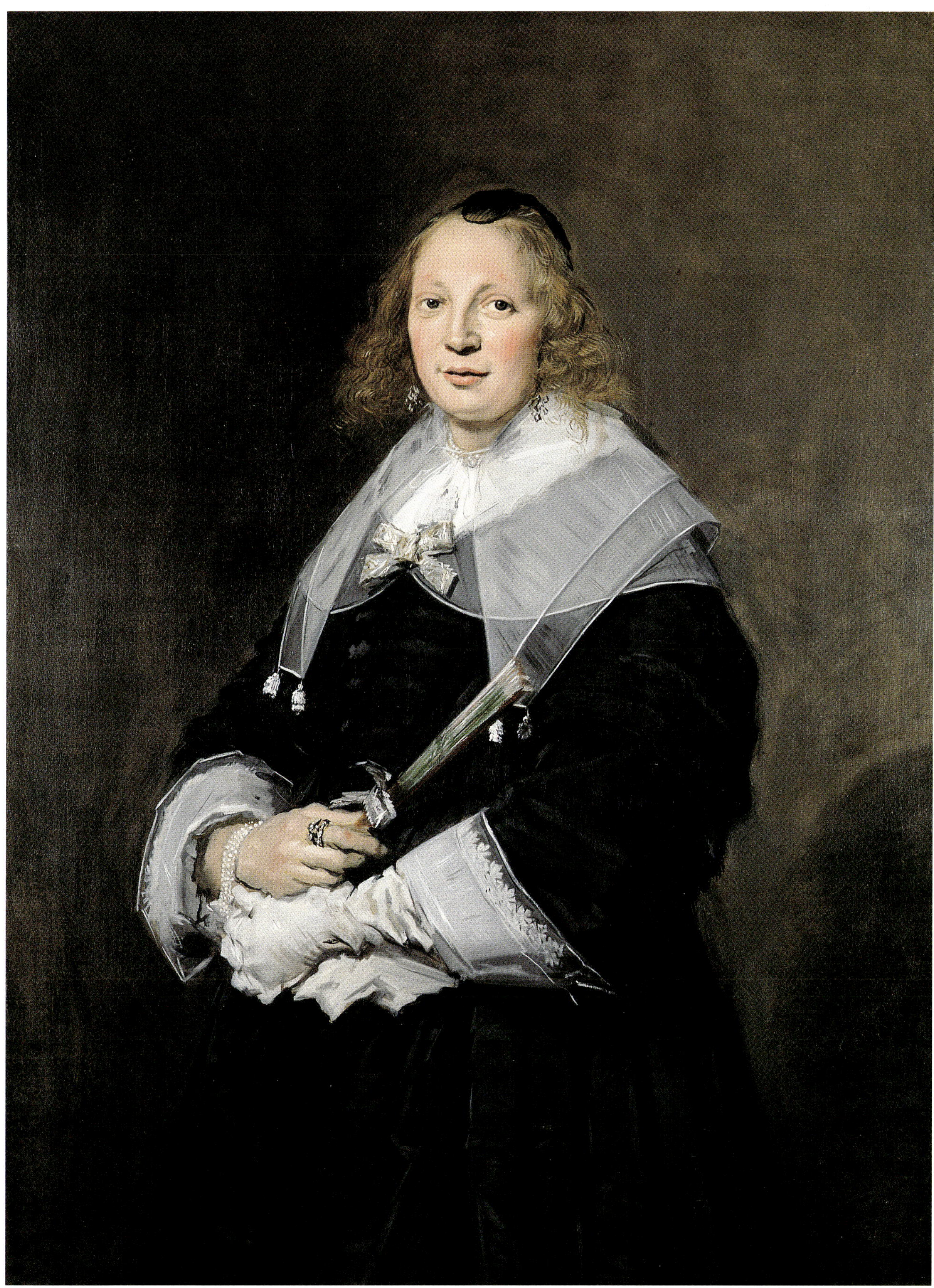

Meindert Hobbema 1638–1709

19 *A Wooded Landscape*, *c.*1662–3

Oil on canvas · 36⅞ × 51½in (93.7 × 130.8cm)
Purchased with the aid of the National Art Collections Fund and the National Heritage Purchase Grant (Scotland) 1979
NG 2377

Hobbema is often considered the last of the great seventeenth-century Dutch landscape painters. He was christened Meindert Lubbertsz. in Amsterdam but adopted the surname Hobbema in his youth for unknown reasons. He trained with the landscape painter Jacob van Ruisdael (*c.*1628/9–82), presumably at some period between Ruisdael settling in Amsterdam in June 1657, and 1660, the year when Ruisdael stated Hobbema had studied with him 'for some years'. Though Hobbema's earliest works seem more to emulate the style of his master's uncle Salomon and the artist Cornelis Vroom, his painting owed a profound debt to Jacob, though, interestingly, this influence did not manifest itself until about 1660. Ruisdael also appears to have been a friend as well as an artistic mentor to Hobbema and he acted as witness to Hobbema's marriage in 1668.

A Wooded Landscape is a mature example of the woodland scenes in which Hobbema specialised. It was painted in *c.*1662–3, at a period when Hobbema had begun to strike out on his own, relying less on Ruisdael's compositions, with a lighter palette and more delicate technique. Though apparently naturalistic, this view was certainly not made from nature and the seeming spontaneity of the composition is, in fact, carefully constructed with its skilful contrast between the darkened foreground and illuminated middle distance. Hobbema produced a number of woodland scenes such as this during the 1660s, built up in a similar way and relating closely to the technique and composition of this work. It seems likely that Hobbema ran a workshop with assistants to complete versions of his compositions and occasionally other artists painted the staffage in his landscapes, though unfortunately nothing specific is known of Hobbema's studio practice.

Hobbema appears to have painted much less towards the latter part of his life and the two latest-dated pictures known, the artist's famous *Avenue at Middelharnis* (National Gallery, London) and the *Landscape with a View of the Bergkerk, Deventer* (Duke of Sutherland loan to the National Gallery of Scotland) both date from the 1680s. This scarcity of late work may be because in 1668 Hobbema married Eeltien Vinck, a kitchen maid to an Amsterdam burgomaster. Probably due to this connection, Hobbema secured a remunerative job that year as a wine-gauger to the Amsterdam *octroi* (tax office) and his production of paintings, no longer his main income, in consequence appears to have dwindled significantly after this. He lived to the age of seventy-one, outlasting his wife and five children and was buried in a pauper's grave in the cemetery of Amsterdam's *Westerkerk* (West Church).

The critic J. T. Smith described *A Wooded Landscape* as 'a capital picture … to be numbered among the artist's most successful productions' in his sixth volume of *Lives and Works of the Most Eminent Dutch, Flemish and French Painters*, London, 1835 (no.27), while Gustaav Waagen praised it for its 'powerful and transparent' effect and the 'cool silvery tones' of the middle ground in his indispensable survey of *Galleries and Cabinets of Art in Great Britain*, London, 1857 (pp.307–8).

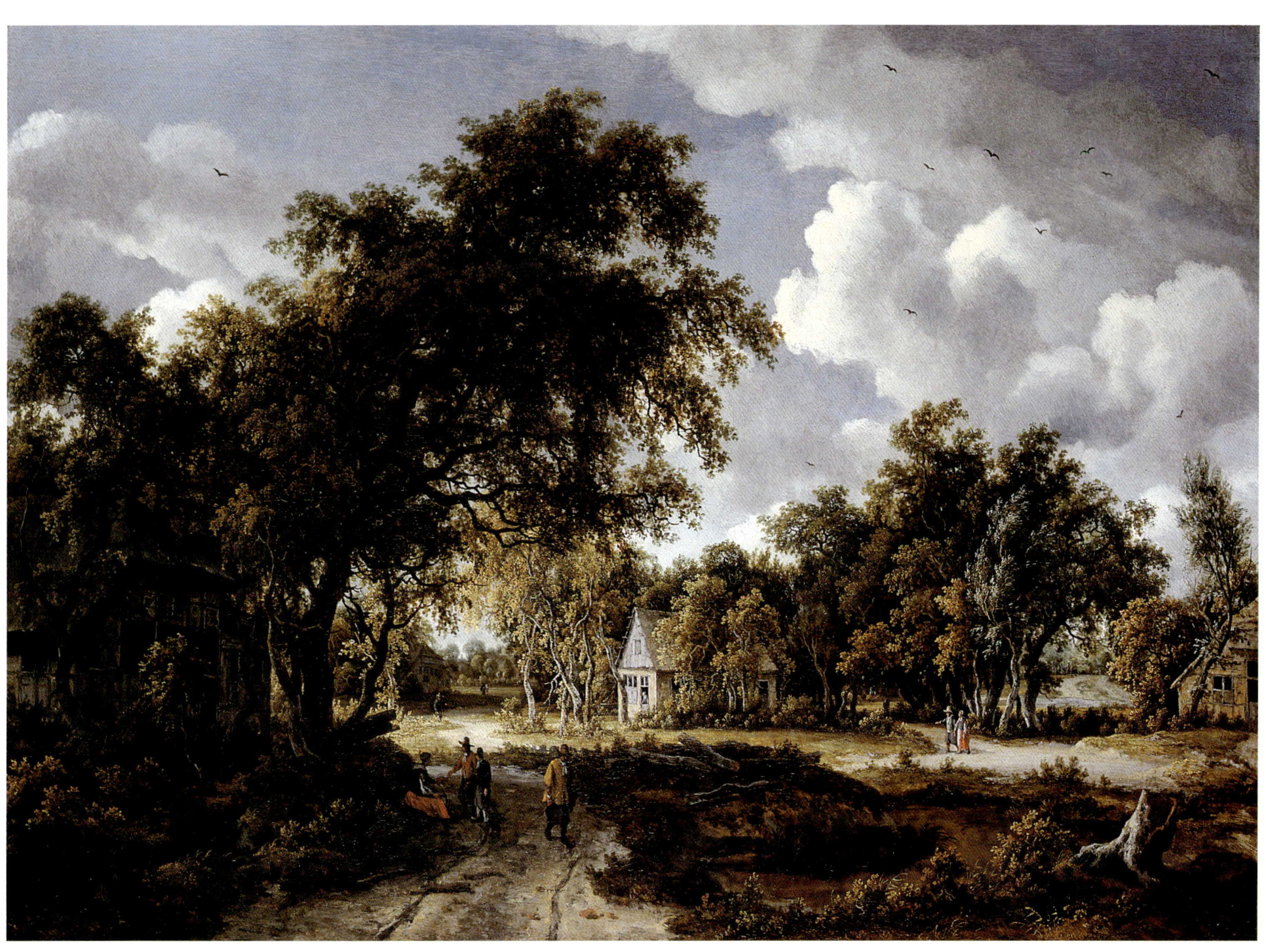

Philips Koninck 1619–1688

20 *An Extensive Landscape*, 1666

Oil on canvas · 35¾ × 44in (91 × 111.8cm)
Signed and dated, lower right: P-koninck 1666
Purchased by Private Treaty 1986
NG 2434

The panorama had been a popular form of landscape in the Low Countries since Pieter Brueghel the Elder, and was developed by Hendrick Goltzius and Hercules Seghers, the last of whom was particularly admired by Koninck and his contemporaries. Koninck gave a new quality to this form, combining imaginary majestic views with more naturalistic vistas. His landscapes evoke the countryside of Gelderland, though, in fact, his works are rarely rooted in topographical accuracy but manage, nonetheless, through their low horizons and large skies, vividly to convey the atmosphere and spirit of the wide Dutch plains.

The 'bird's-eye view' so effectively used here means that the onlooker looks down on the foreground, while the horizon spreads out below and beyond. The viewer's vantage point is actually up amongst the strongly-defined fleecy clouds which flock the sky, so characteristic of Koninck's work at this period. The one element of high ground within the picture, prominent through its central position and the light catching its bright green contours, gives some relief to the receding flatter landscape, but not so much that it throws the remaining composition out of balance. The Edinburgh work shows strong similarities with two other, slightly earlier pictures – *Panoramic Landscape* 1665 (J. Paul Getty Museum, Los Angeles) and the *Panoramic Landscape with Fishermen c.*1665 (Hunterian Art Gallery, Glasgow). The Edinburgh painting was on loan at the Fitzwilliam Museum, Cambridge, for some years, but was unpublished before its acquisition for the National Gallery of Scotland in 1986.

Philips Koninck was born in Amsterdam and was related to a family of goldsmiths and painters. He was apprenticed to his brother Jacob in Rotterdam for about three years from 1637. There he met his first wife, the daughter of a Rotterdam surgeon, whom he married in 1641. Her brother was Abraham Furnerius, a pupil of Rembrandt, whose drawings strongly resemble those of Koninck. There is no documented proof that Koninck also became a pupil of Rembrandt's when he returned to Amsterdam in 1642, but records note that Rembrandt sold Koninck a pearl necklace in about 1651 so they certainly knew each other by then. It has been suggested that the two artists were friends and may have sketched outdoors together (more than 300 drawings by Koninck have survived). They would have shared an admiration for the work of Seghers (by whom Rembrandt owned eight paintings and numerous prints) and Koninck's work undoubtedly shows knowledge of Rembrandt's landscapes of the 1640s, especially his prints.

Being of independent means through his second marriage (through ownership of lucrative ferry services), Koninck could afford to concentrate on his landscapes though history paintings and portraits by him are also known. He appears to have stopped painting in about 1676, but he was still frequently consulted as an expert on authentication of pictures, and his reputation was sufficiently high for his *Self-portrait* of 1667 to be bought by Cosimo III de' Medici for the Artists' Gallery in the Uffizi, Florence, where it still hangs.

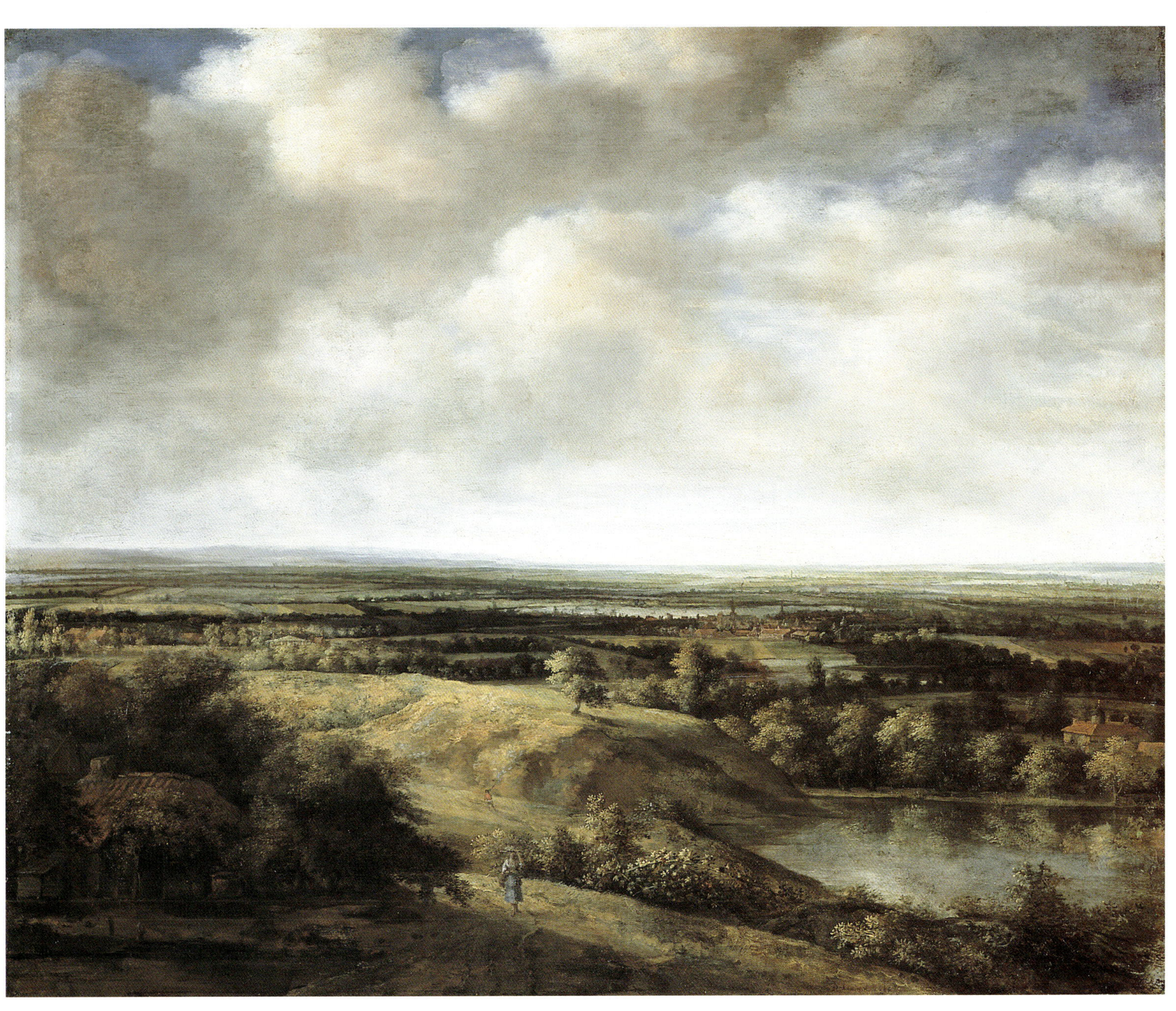

Jan Steen 1625/26–1679

21 *A School for Boys and Girls, c.1670*

Oil on canvas · 32⅛ × 42¾in (81.7 × 108.6cm)
Purchased by Private Treaty with the aid of the National Heritage Memorial Fund 1984
NG 2421

Jan Steen was born in Leiden and was enrolled as a student of the university there in 1646. However, he became a Leiden guild painter by 1648, having trained with the landscape artist Jan van Goyen in The Hague, with Nicholas Knüpfer in Utrecht and Adriaen van Ostade in Haarlem. Steen painted some portraits, biblical and mythological paintings but is best known for his genre scenes of rowdy life. His practice of including his own portrait in many such scenes and the fact that he ran a tavern and was frequently impecunious, have conspired to create a somewhat fictionalised character for the artist. The critic Arnold Houbraken (1660–1719) wrote that Steen's 'paintings are as his way of life and his way of life as his paintings'. Even today the contemporary Dutch phrase 'a Jan Steen household' signifies a messy disorganised home full of mayhem. This idea of the artist as always drunk and in disarray is, however, distinctly at odds with his careful painting and intelligently wry comedy displayed in works such as the *School for Girls and Boys.*

This is the largest of several schoolroom scenes by Steen and was painted in about 1670. An earlier, less elaborate, composition is in the National Gallery of Ireland, Dublin, and a related picture is in a private collection (see *Jan Steen; Painter and Storyteller*, exhibition catalogue, National Gallery of Art, Washington and Rijksmuseum, Amsterdam, 1996–7, cat.nos.35 and 41). The theme of the unruly school had previously been depicted by artists such as Pieter Brueghel and Isack and Adriaen van Ostade but Steen clearly took a certain amount of glee in portraying the evils of inattentiveness in a school without discipline. In fact, although Dutch children were often considered unruly and spoilt, contemporary records show that the level of literacy was comparatively high for Europe. Children were expected to learn by rote and were also given individual work, senior pupils helping the younger ones as seen here with the little group of girls in the left foreground. The objects hanging on the end wall of the room are the childrens' school boxes but they are presumably not much used, for here the pandemonium wrought by the pupils is studiously ignored by the schoolmaster and his wife who make no attempt to regain order. A print of Hans Holbein's portrait of the great scholar Erasmus of Rotterdam is pointedly discarded under the bench at the right. A small boy offers a pair of spectacles to the owl perched near a lamp, acting out a Dutch proverb: 'What is the need for a candle or glasses if the owl cannot and does not want to see?' (roughly paralleled by the saying 'You can lead a horse to water...'). Ironically, the owl was also recognised as a symbol of wisdom, the attribute of the goddess Athena. Continuing such learned allusions, Steen loosely based the whole of the design for his picture on Raphael's composition of the *School of Athens* (*La Disputa*) in the Vatican. It is the artist's erudite joke to base such classroom chaos on the dignified grouping of the greatest scholars of antiquity.

The painting was in the collection of the important Dutch eighteenth-century timber merchant and connoisseur Gerrit Braamcamp, who lived at 462 Herengracht, one of the expensively elegant canal houses in Amsterdam. The sale of this remarkable collection of paintings, drawings, prints and sculptures after his death in 1771 was a spectacular event with 318 paintings of exceptionally high quality sold, of which six works were by Jan Steen. The picture was later bought for Lord Francis Egerton, 1st Earl of Ellesmere (1800–1857), and inheritor of the extraordinary Bridgewater House collection from his great uncle the 3rd Duke of Bridgewater, and was purchased from his descendants by the Gallery in 1984.

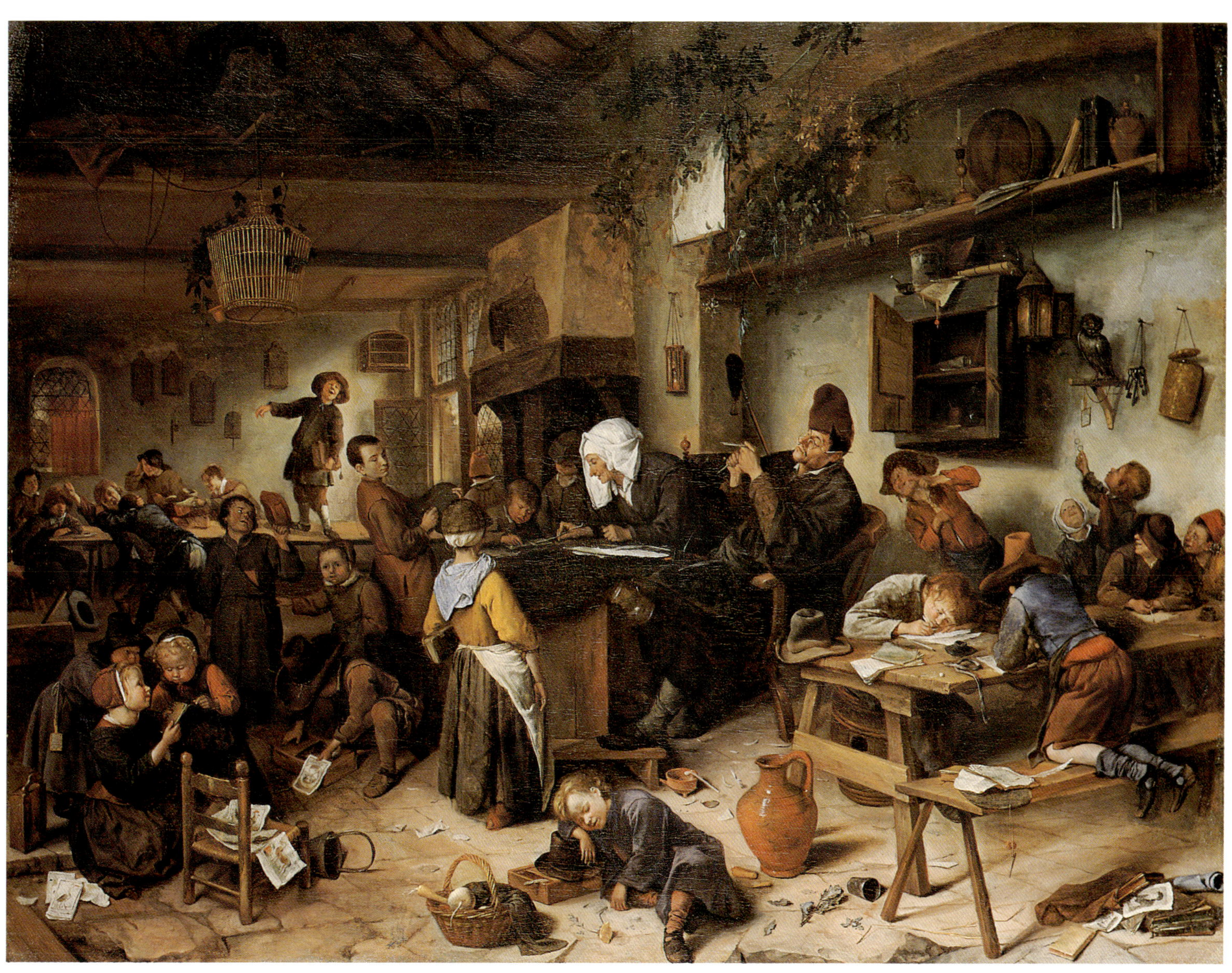

Emanuel De Witte 1615/17–1691/2

22 *The Interior of a Dutch Church, c.1680*

Oil on canvas · 74¾ × 63¾in (190 × 162cm)
Purchased 1909
NG 990

This painting, the largest of De Witte's to have survived, is one of a series of partially imaginary interiors which incorporate elements from both the *Oudekerk* and *Nieuwekerk* (Old Church and New Church) in Amsterdam. The interior resembles the latter, but the columns are from the *Oudekerk*, while the somewhat simplified decoration on the capitals is an invention of the artist. Here he shows his mastery in the depiction of still space punctuated by scattered sunlight across the huge columns. It has been suggested that the woman sitting on the left suckling her child is an allegorical reference to Charity, or to the Virgin and Child, though this may be far fetched as De Witte included nursing mothers in many of his other compositions. The wheelbarrow full of soil, dug for a new grave while the former occupant's skull is cast on the flagstones might, equally, refer to the frailty of human life. However, the dog at the right relieving itself on a pillar does not necessarily fit easily into such an interpretation and it is just as likely that De Witte was simply filling his scene with vivid observations of daily life. Such behaviour might now be regarded as disrespectful in a place of worship but, in fact, contemporary records note that it was far from unusual for some people to use their church as a general meeting place and even a dog-walking venue if the weather was inclement.

A smaller version formerly in a private collection in Enschede (see Haboldt and Co., *Catalogue des Tableaux Anciens*, Paris, 1990–1, cat.no.17) shows virtually the same view. This work is signed and dated 1679 but the larger Edinburgh canvas probably dates from the following year (see *Perspectives: Saenredam and the architectural painters of the 17th century*, exhibition catalogue, Boijmans Van Beuningen Museum, Rotterdam, 1991, cat.no.40). The sheer size of the Edinburgh *Interior of a Dutch Church* has led to the plausible speculation that it may have been a specific commission, though for which patron or purpose is unknown. Another smaller work now at the Rijksmuseum, Amsterdam (Acc.no.2697), shows the reverse view from the south transept looking north.

De Witte is known as one of the last and most proficient Dutch church painters of the seventeenth century but he also produced some market scenes, landscapes and townscapes. He actually started his career working on biblical and mythological scenes and did not concentrate upon church painting until after 1650. Emanuel was born in Alkmaar, but he trained in Delft, probably with Evert van Aelst (1602–1657) who was a still-life painter in the city. Delft was a famous centre for architectural painting though De Witte's concentration on interior perspectives was perhaps influenced by the fact that his father was a schoolmaster who taught him the art of geometry, according to the eighteenth-century critic and art historian Arnold Houbraken. Houbraken also noted that Emanuel was 'inclined to brag about his knowledge of geometry' but, intriguingly, the paintings do not demonstrate a significant grasp of the theories of perspective until about 1660. He joined the artists' guild in his native Alkmaar in 1636, but lived in Delft and Rotterdam before moving to Amsterdam in about 1652. De Witte was apparently prone to fits of depression which culminated in his probable suicide in the winter of 1691/2, all the more poignant in view of his success in portraying tranquil church interiors such as this.

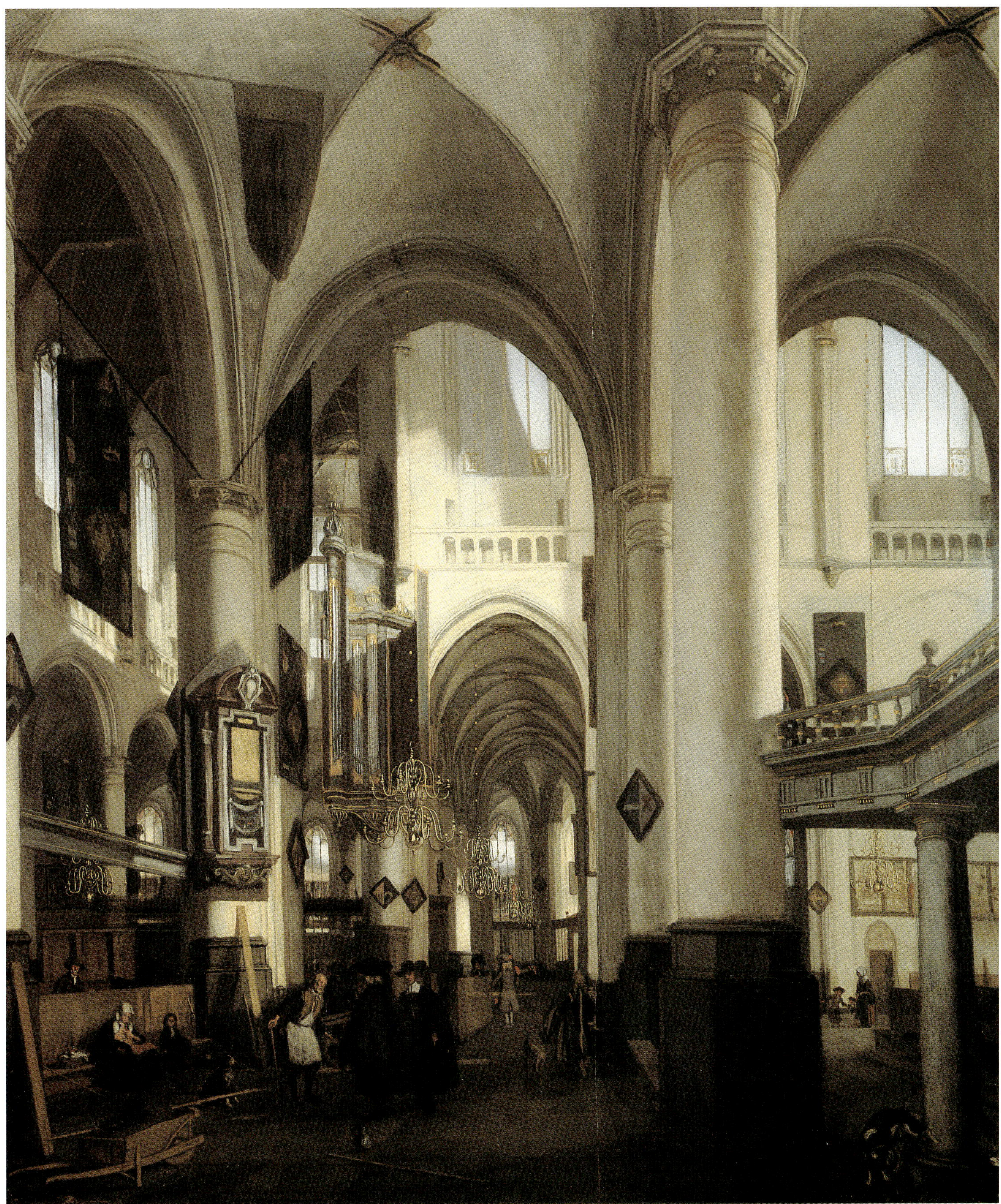

Godfried Schalcken 1643–1706

23 *A Boy Blowing on a Firebrand to Light a Candle*, c.1692–8

Oil on canvas · 29½ × 25in (75 × 63.5cm)
Purchased with the aid of the National Art Collections Fund
and the National Heritage Memorial Fund 1989
NG 2495

Schalcken was the son of the minister of the parish of Made near Dordrecht. He became a pupil between 1656 and 1662 of the Dordrecht artist Samuel van Hoogstraten, who had trained with Rembrandt in the 1640s. Schalcken then moved to the university town of Leiden to work for Gerrit Dou. Dou was also a former pupil of Rembrandt, but was by this time renowned for the meticulous style he had made his own, 'Fine-painting', which, brushstroke by seamless brushstroke, rendered the sheen upon satin and shine upon silver so strikingly. By 1665 Schalcken had returned to Dordrecht and was registered as being an ensign in a militia company there. He paid dues to an artists' guild in The Hague in 1691 but then left for Britain in about 1692, returning to the Netherlands in 1698. He settled in The Hague, where he became a citizen in 1699, and remained there until his death, apart from working in Düsseldorf for the Elector Palatine, Johann Wilhelm, in about 1703.

Though Schalcken started painting with the painstaking precision of his master Dou's '*fijnschilder*' (fine-painter) technique, he later abandoned this style but continued to be captivated by Dou's treatment of artificial light. Despite painting portraits, genre pictures and some religious and mythological subjects (many set in daylight), it is for night scenes that Schalcken is best known. *A Boy Blowing on a Firebrand to Light a Candle* may be an example of *ekphrasis* (the re-creation of works of art described in classical sources), for it appears to relate to a passage in the classical author Pliny the Elder's *Natural History* (XXXV, 138). Pliny describes a painting by the ancient Greek artist Antiphilus of Alexandria, a 'Boy Blowing on Fire ... beautiful in itself, lit by the reflection from the fire and the light thrown on the boy's face'.

A painting by El Greco, *Boy Blowing on a Candle* (Museo di Capodimonte, Naples) is one of the earliest compositions to focus solely upon the figure of the boy blowing on fire, probably inspired by the classical leanings of the erudite Farnese family in whose Roman palace the picture hung until 1622. It would almost certainly have been seen there by the Dutch painters Hendrick ter Brugghen (1588–1629) and Gerrit Honthorst (1590–1656) during their respective Italian visits in the first and second decades of the seventeenth century for they, too, created similar compositions at this time. These were emulated by other Northern artists, giving an opportunity to display their technical mastery of the portrayal of light and shadow. Such a figure shown blowing on a firebrand or candle also often appears to have had allegorical significance. When painted by Jan Lievens (1607–1674), the scene represented *Fire*, *c.*1624–6 (as one of four paintings of *The Elements*), but generally it referred to a 'hot' temper or 'fiery' lust, related to a contemporary saying, 'Blowing a burning coal makes a flame, and an ill word excites anger', or proverbs warning against becoming inflamed with heated desire.

Schalcken painted a number of such nocturnal scenes with men or women blowing zestfully upon flames and embers, sometimes with figures in the background making obscene gestures to accentuate such lecherous connotations. However, this version is more restrained and closer in type, perhaps, to Antiphilus's original example. The painting came from Althorp (home of Earl Spencer) where it was seen and admired by Horace Walpole and George Vertue, the latter of whom remarked of the boy, 'Striving to Blow the Brand into Flame, brightens his own face, and the Author's Fame' (Note Book, 1731–6, British Museum, BM Add.Ms 23071). The picture was probably commissioned for Robert Spencer, 2nd Earl of Sunderland, during Schalcken's British sojourn.

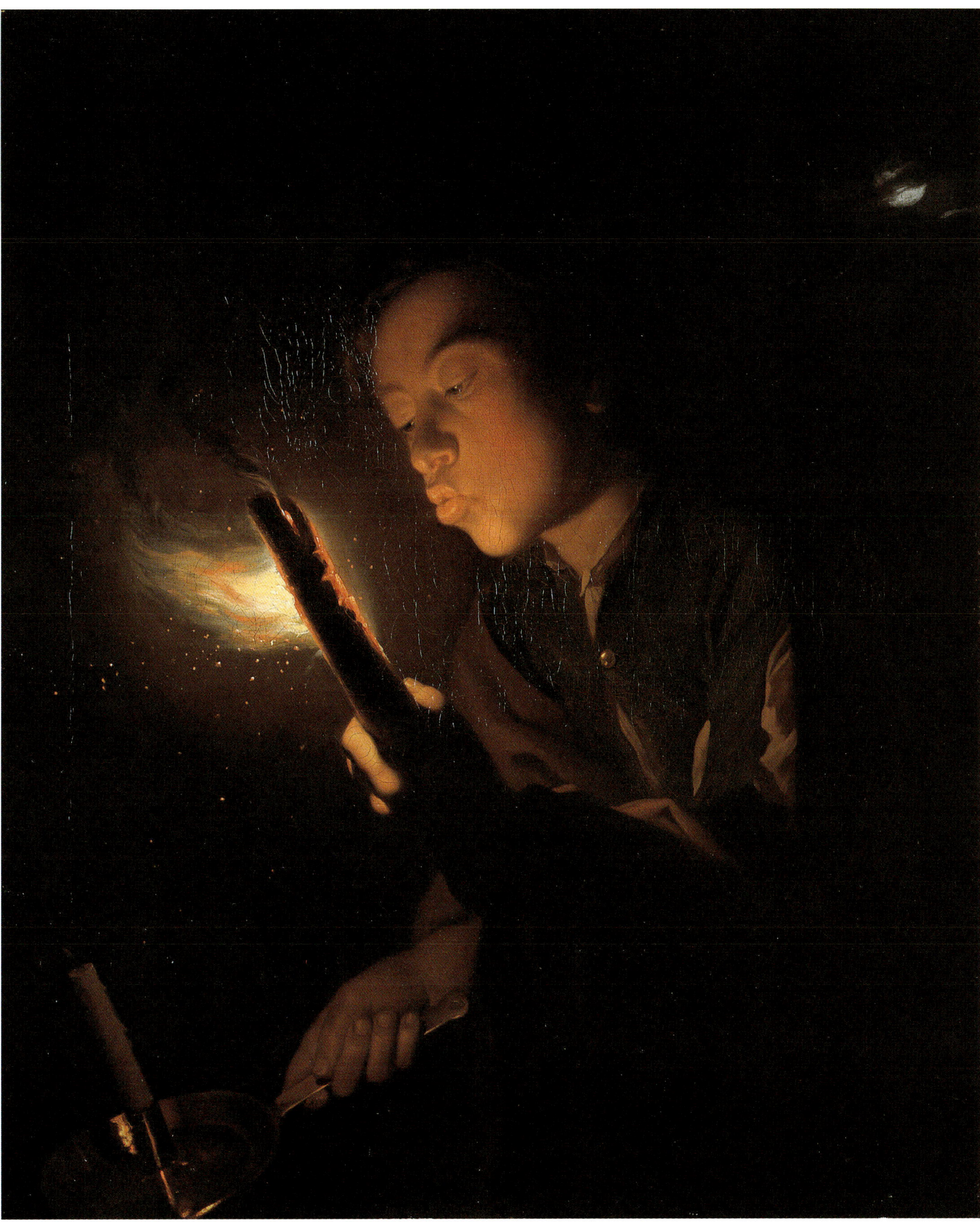

Gaspard Dughet, called Gaspard Poussin 1615–1675

24 *Classical Landscape with a Lake*, 1660s

Oil on canvas · 28¾ × 39in (73 × 99cm)
Purchased 1973
NG 2318

Born in Rome to a French father and an Italian mother, Gaspard adopted the name of Poussin from his brother-in-law Nicolas Poussin (1594–1665), of whom he was a pupil and who had married his sister Anne-Marie. His work combines aspects of the landscapes of his great contemporaries, Poussin and Claude Lorrain, though Gaspard rarely included human figures for anything more than decorative effect – his landscapes contain few narratives. On occasion he favoured a wilder, rougher kind of nature than Claude or Poussin. Gaspard never left Italy but his most notable absences from Rome included a visit to Florence and a prolonged stay in Naples in the 1640s. Some of Gaspard's most important works date from the last two decades of his life and include decorative cycles for the Palazzo Colonna and Palazzo Borghese in Rome.

Gaspard's paintings proved highly popular with British Grand Tourists in the eighteenth century who brought them back from Italy to decorate their town and country houses, often using them as overdoors. His work influenced a number of British artists, notably the Welsh landscape painter Richard Wilson (1713/14–1782), and he was also highly regarded by the theorists and landscape gardeners of the Picturesque movement in the latter half of the eighteenth century.

The dating of Gaspard's landscapes is problematic and this exceptionally beautiful example of his work has been variously dated between the 1640s and 1660s (see M.-N. Boisclair *Gaspard Dughet 1615–1675*, Paris, 1986, cat.no.286, fig.325). The attribution to Gaspard, which there seems no good reason to doubt, is on grounds of style, though it has recently been suggested by Clovis Whitfield ('A propos des paysages de Poussin', *Nicolas Poussin (1594–1665)*, Paris, 1996, I, pp.252–5) that the picture may be by Nicolas Poussin. This hypothesis is based on stylistic comparison with Poussin's pair of landscapes painted for Pointel in the 1640s, the *Storm* (Musée des Beaux-Arts, Rouen), and, in particular, the *Calm* (J. Paul Getty Museum, Los Angeles). The most probable solution is that this is a late work by Gaspard (whose characteristic colouring it retains), but heavily influenced by the classical balance of composition Nicolas Poussin achieved in his own landscapes.

The picture may have belonged to Alfred Buckley (son-in-law of Lord Radnor), who lent the following work by Gaspard to the 1883 Royal Academy Old Masters exhibition in London, '190 … Right: a pool and trees beyond. Left: buildings with a fisherman and a dog. Sheep near the pool. In the left foreground, a female figure with a boy.' In addition, its recorded measurements were very close to those of the Edinburgh canvas. By 1960 it was in the collection of Mrs R.D.M. Thesiger, from which it was purchased by the Gallery thirteen years later.

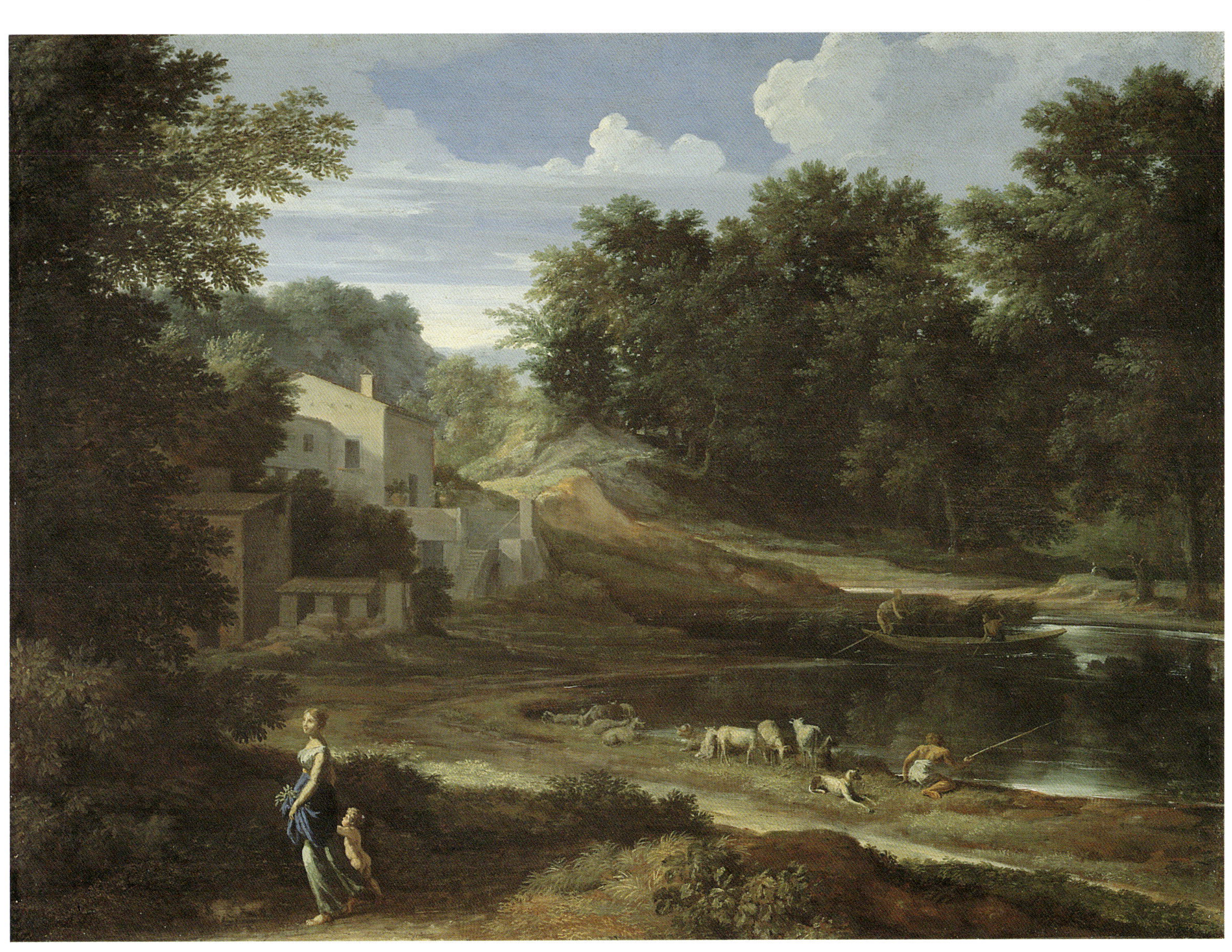

Jean-Antoine Watteau 1684–1721

25 *The Robber of the Sparrow's Nest*, *c.*1711–12

Oil on paper laid on canvas on panel · 8⅞ × 7¼in (22.6 × 18.5cm)
Presented by Mrs Hugh William Williams 1860
NG 370

Watteau was born in Valenciennes, a town which had only recently been ceded to France from the Spanish Netherlands. Although regarded by his contemporaries as a Flemish artist, he is now considered the greatest French painter of the Rococo, that light, elegant and sensuous style which dominated French art in the first half of the eighteenth century. Watteau arrived in Paris *c.*1702 and worked with Claude Gillot and, perhaps more importantly, Claude Audran, Keeper of the Luxembourg Palace, which housed Rubens's great decorative cycle of the history of Marie de Médicis. Rubens's art was highly influential upon Watteau, not least by dint of its frequent portrayal of subjects related to the theme of the Garden of Love. But whereas Rubens's figures are robust and bursting with energy and vitality, those of Watteau are fragile, wistful and often suffused with a gentle melancholy. Watteau devised a special category of picture, the 'fête galante', in which young people, exquisitely dressed, idle their time away in dreamy and romantic pastoral settings. It was as a painter of this specific type of picture that Watteau was admitted into the French Academy in 1717, his reception piece being *The Pilgrimage to the Island of Cythera* (Louvre, Paris).

This charming, relatively early work, normally dated to 1711–12, depicts a boy showing a girl a bird's nest he has just taken from a tree. It is probably cut down and originally measured 14⅞ × 10⅛ (the size recorded when it was in the Jean de Jullienne collection). The whole composition was engraved in reverse (perhaps with additional arabesque embellishments) by F. Boucher for de Jullienne's *L'Oeuvre d'Antoine Watteau*, 1734. Traces of decorative swags at the top and a stone cartouche at the bottom, corresponding to the engraving, are visible under later over-painting.

Such decorative work is testament to Watteau's earlier training and to his collaboration with Audran, who was an experienced ornamentalist and purveyor of graceful arabesques that characterise so much Rococo decoration. Watteau had often assisted Audran with his designs by adding the figures. The range of Watteau's own decorative work was very considerable and embraced designs for ceilings, boiserie, tapestries, screens, fans, bookplates and even coach doors. It has been suggested that this particular painting may have been a shop sign for Watteau's dealer at this time, Sirois, but its small size would appear to rule out this possibility.

The picture was one of the very first gifts to the National Gallery of Scotland and was presented in 1860 by Mrs Hugh William Williams, widow of the artist Hugh 'Grecian' William Williams (1773–1829), so-called after his many watercolours of Greece and the Near East, who was highly regarded by no less a landscape painter than J. M.W. Turner. Williams settled in Edinburgh and knowledge there of his views of Greece may well have been influential on the extensive building programme undertaken in the city which came to be known as the 'Athens of the North'.

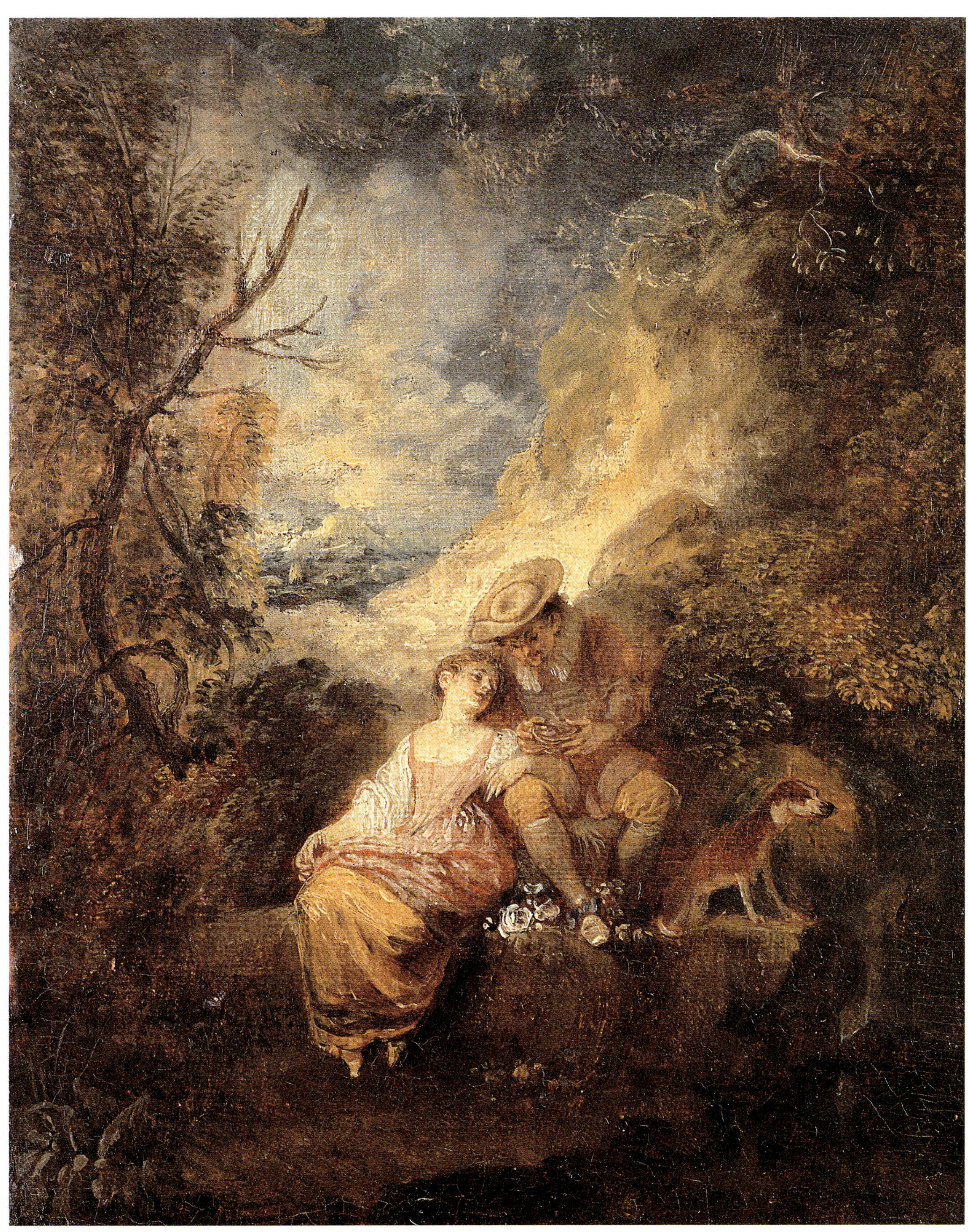

Jean-Siméon Chardin 1699–1779

26 *Still Life: The Kitchen Table*, 1730s

Oil on canvas · 16 × 12¾in (40.6 × 32.4cm)
Signed, on the table edge to the right of the cloth: j.s.chardin.
Purchased 1908
NG 959

One of the greatest of all still-life painters, Chardin occupied an unusual position in the complex hierarchy of French eighteenth-century art. In 1728 he was received into the French Academy as a painter of 'animals and fruit' and, from the mid-1750s until near the end of his life, he was responsible for the organising and hanging of the (usually) annual exhibitions of the Academy at the Paris Salon. Extremely popular with contemporary collectors and hailed by the foremost art critic of his day, Denis Diderot, as a 'great magician, with your silent compositions!', Chardin suffered posthumous neglect. His unassuming art was seemingly incompatible with the stern morality and complex figurative compositions of Neoclassicism, the style which dominated French art at the end of the eighteenth and beginning of the nineteenth centuries. It was only towards the middle of the nineteenth century that he was rediscovered by Realist critics such as Théophile Thoré (who was also the principal agent in the 'rediscovery' of Vermeer around this time) and subsequently influenced a whole host of Realist still-life painters. Chardin's scenes of everyday life (of which fine examples in Scotland can be found in the Hunterian Art Gallery, University of Glasgow) also had a profound effect on such major nineteenth-century artists as Millet and Courbet.

Chardin painted still lifes throughout his career. This particular example has been dated by various authorities to two distinctly different phases in Chardin's career. The majority opinion favours a relatively early date in the 1730s, and comparisons have been drawn with a number of pictures which feature similar items, particularly the *Still Life of Kitchen Utensils* in the Ashmolean Museum, Oxford. However, after the picture had been included in the great Chardin exhibition of 1979 (*Chardin*, Grand Palais, Paris; Cleveland Museum of Art; Museum of Fine Arts, Boston cat.no.44), it was later suggested by Pierre Rosenberg (*Tout l'oeuvre peint de Chardin*, Milan, 1983, no.141), that it should instead be grouped on grounds of style with other pictures of the 1750s, a period when Chardin showed a renewed interest in the category of still life.

The picture's later owners included Alexis Vollon, son of the well-known still-life painter Antoine Vollon (1833–1900), who was known as the 'Chardin of the nineteenth century'.

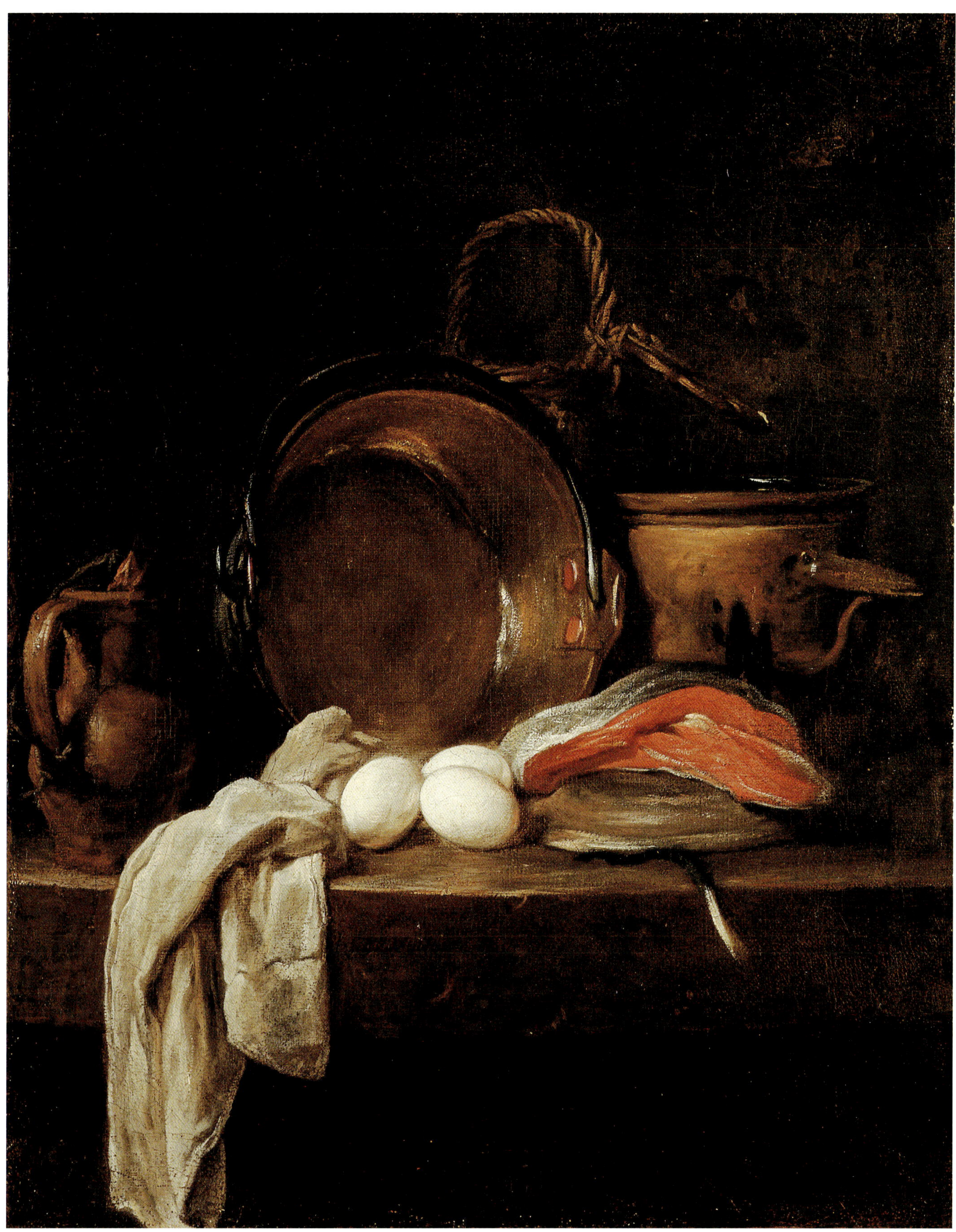

François Boucher 1703–1770

27 *Madame de Pompadour*, late 1750s?

Oil on canvas · 14¼ × 17½in (36.2 × 44.5cm)
Bequest of Lady Murray of Henderland 1861
NG 429

Born in Paris, Boucher probably trained with his father and then with François Lemoyne. He was awarded the Prix de Rome in 1724 and was received by the French Academy as a history painter in 1734. Immensely prolific, his decorative panels and mythological paintings epitomised French painting around the middle of the eighteenth century. He also created tapestry cartoons for the Beauvais and Gobelins manufactories, porcelain designs for Sèvres and sets and costumes for the theatre. Widely employed by the French monarchy, he benefited in particular from the installation of Madame de Pompadour as Louis XV's official mistress in 1745. He was appointed First Painter to the King in 1765.

Jeanne Antoinette Poisson (1721–1764), the subject of this picture, was made Louis XV's 'Maîtresse en titre' (his official mistress) and Marquise de Pompadour in 1745. She exerted considerable influence on the artistic life of the period. The Edinburgh picture is a reduction of the great 1756 whole-length of her by Boucher, now on deposit from the Bayerische Hypotheken and Wechselbank to the Alte Pinakothek, Munich (A. Ananoff and D. Wildenstein *François Boucher*, Lausanne and Paris, 1976, II, no.475). It was in 1756 that Madame de Pompadour was officially named as a 'dame du Palais' of Louis's Queen, Marie Leczinka. The Munich portrait, which was exhibited at the Paris Salon of 1757 on its own dais, may therefore have been commissioned as an official celebration of Madame de Pompadour's transition from carnal to purely titular mistress of the King. In it the marquise is depicted in an elaborate dress, surrounded by books and fine furniture. The Edinburgh reduction, however, omits the library and shows the marquise against a plain background setting and only in half length. In addition, there are traces of squaring-up visible under the paint surface. The purpose of this is unclear for squaring-up is normally used for aiding the transfer of images of equal size or from a smaller sketch to a larger picture. The handling of the Edinburgh picture, though extremely beautiful, is bright and detailed, rather unlike Boucher's characteristically looser and more painterly touch. For these reasons, it has been suggested that the Edinburgh version might originate from Boucher's studio or from an as yet unidentified but rather distinctive painter associated with Boucher.

This picture formed part of one of the earliest bequests to the newly established National Gallery of Scotland, arriving two years after it first opened to the public in 1859. Lady Murray had lived with her late husband in Great Stuart Street, Edinburgh and they had inherited a major part of the pictures and drawings collected by General John Ramsay, son of the distinguished Scottish painter Allan Ramsay (1713–1784, see no.34). Widely travelled, John Ramsay had visited many of the major European capitals, had studied briefly with such famous artists as Pompeo Batoni, and was a collector of ancient bronzes, marbles, Etruscan pottery and pictures. He was especially fond of Dutch and Flemish paintings, as well as those of the French eighteenth-century school, and with the Murray of Henderland Bequest the Gallery received eight paintings in the latter category, including this painting, the great Watteau *Fêtes Vénitiennes* and four works by or attributed to Greuze (see no.28).

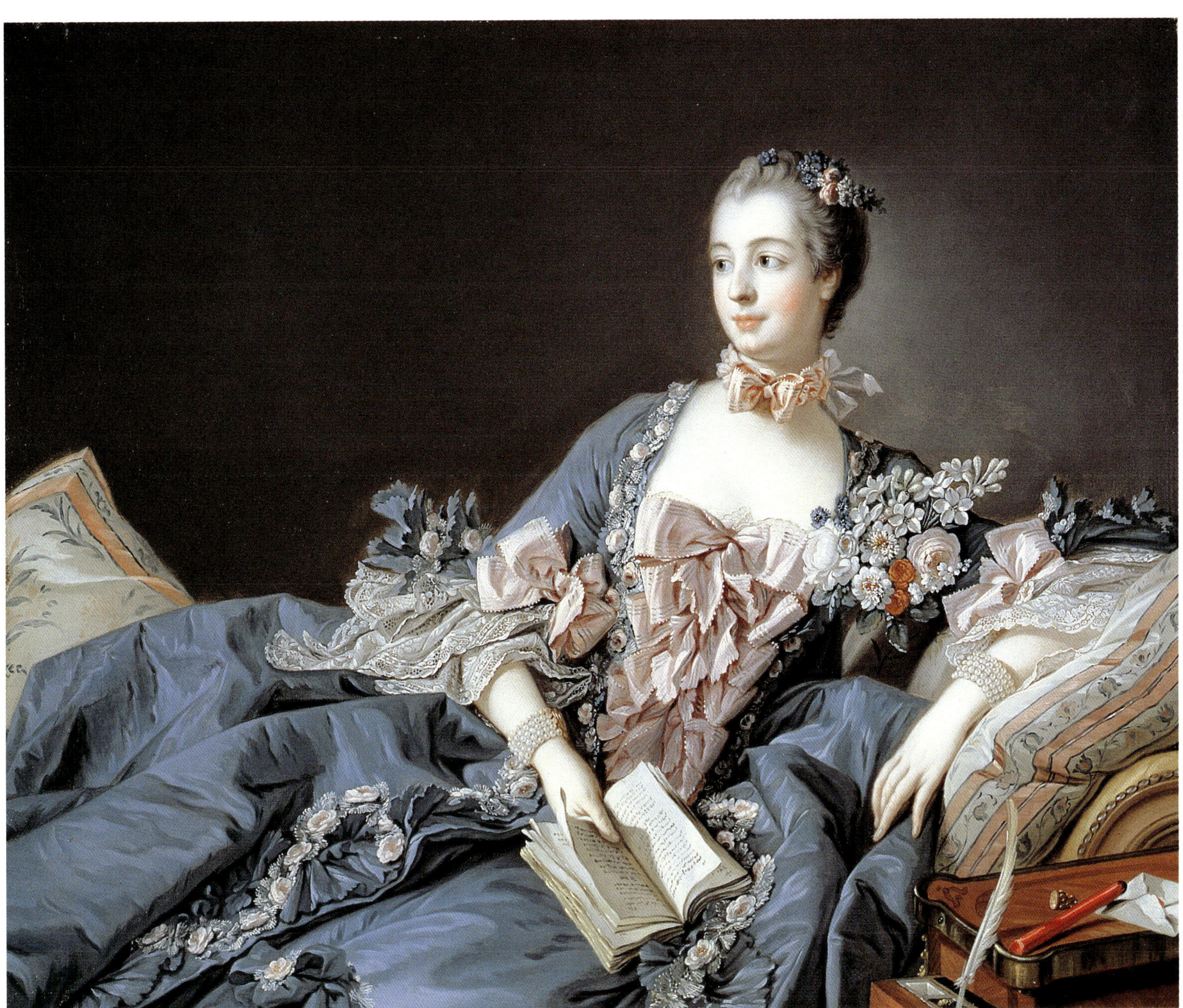

Jean-Baptiste Greuze 1725–1805

28 *A Boy with a Lesson-book*, 1756–7

Oil on canvas · 24½ × 19¼in (62.5 × 49cm)
Bequest of Lady Murray of Henderland 1861
NG 436

Greuze enjoyed great popularity in the period between the Rococo and Neoclassicism as a painter of sentimental and melodramatic genre scenes, in which the potentially devastating tragedies of family life were played out. Their moralising content attracted the admiration of many critics, most notably Denis Diderot. Greuze's attempts to translate his morality tales into the sterner world of neoclassical history painting were less successful, however. He ceased to exhibit at the Paris Salon after taking offence at being accepted into the French Academy in 1769 only as a genre rather than as a history painter. His studio became his place of exhibition and among the visitors he received there was Emperor Joseph II, Marie-Antoinette's brother. In fact, he commanded his highest prices in the period immediately after his perceived snub by the Academy and his fortunes only waned after the arrival on the Parisian art scene of Jacques-Louis David in the 1780s.

Greuze had risen to public prominence with the many favourable critical notices accorded to his submissions to the 1755 Salon. Buoyed by this success he was in Italy from 1755 to 1757 and apparently executed this picture at the end of his stay there, exhibiting it back in Paris at the 1757 Salon (no.119). It depicts a boy committing a text to memory, his hand placed over the book he is memorising. His unusual coiffure, with the hair pulled up into a central braid, was probably adapted from that found in a marble bust by the sculptor Jacques Saly (1717–1776) of the daughter of the painter Jean-François de Troy (at that time Director of the French Academy in Rome), which he exhibited at the 1750 Salon and was known in many versions. Although painted in Italy, this moving picture, a study in concentration, shows the strong influence of Dutch seventeenth-century painting and, in its subtle brown tonalities, of Rembrandt in particular. It is reminiscent of Rembrandt's treatment of a similar subject in his *Portrait of Titus at his Desk* (Museum Boijmans Van Beuningen, Rotterdam). A related picture by Greuze, dating from probably two years earlier, depicts *A Boy Fallen Asleep over his Lesson-book* and is now in the Musée Fabre, Montpellier.

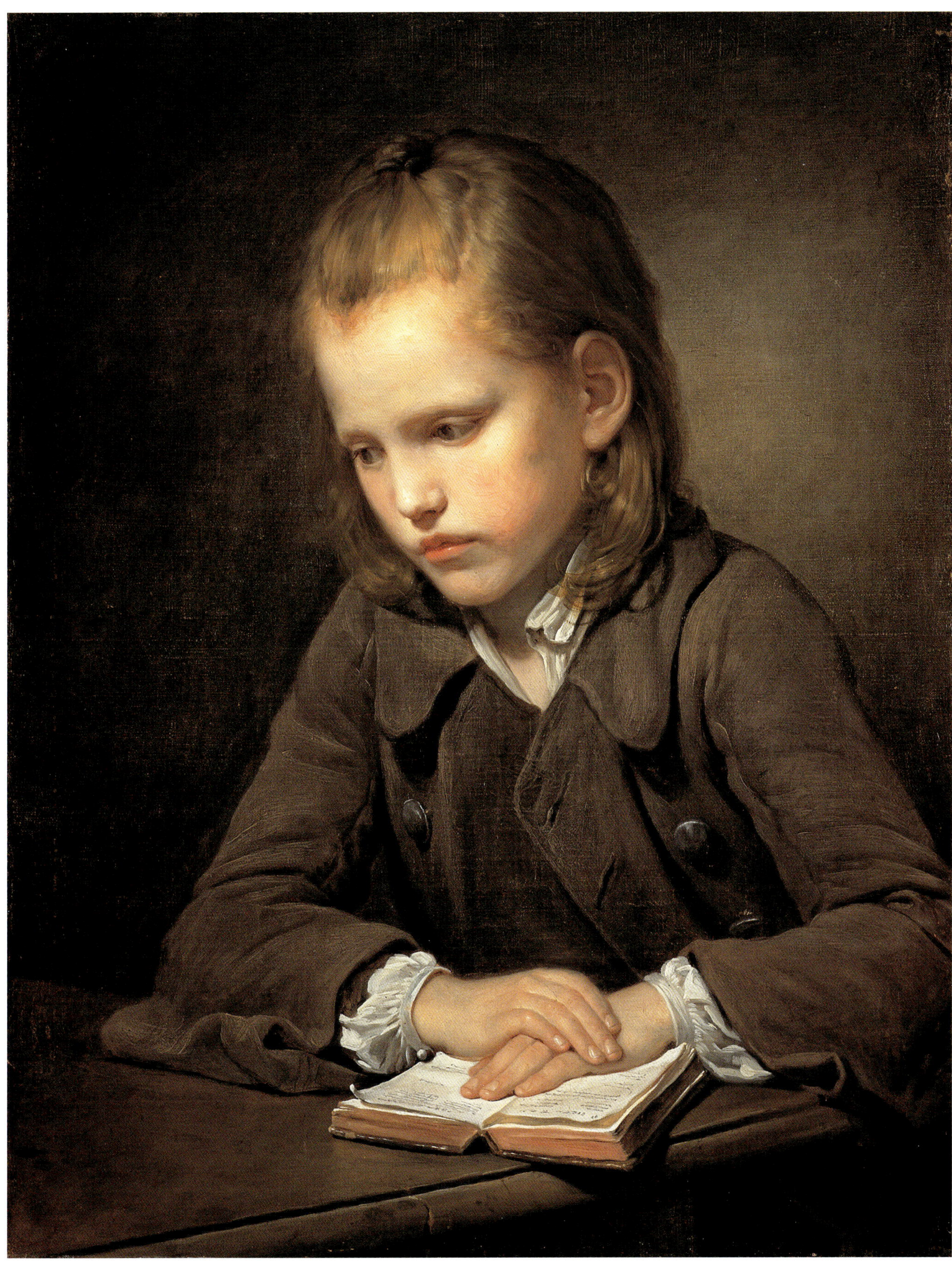

Louis Gauffier 1761–1801

29 *Cleopatra and Octavian*, 1787–8

Oil on canvas · 33 × 44¼in (83.8 × 112.5cm)
Purchased with the aid of the National Art Collections Fund 1991
NG 2526

Gauffier was one of a number of French neoclassical artists who spent most of their careers in Italy. He first went there in 1784 as a joint winner, with Jean-Germain Drouais, of the Prix de Rome for that year. Except for a brief return to Paris in 1789, he remained in Rome until 1793 when, in common with other French artists resident there, he was forced by anti-French feelings after the execution of Louis XVI to remove to Florence, together with his young wife, his former pupil Pauline Chatillon. In Florence he painted portraits and conversation pieces of the European aristocracy who had settled there, and he also took an increasing interest in landscape painting. In the later 1790s he painted a celebrated set of views of the monastery of Vallombrosa, situated up in the Apeninnes near the source of the Arno. In 1801 he was called back to Paris but died en route at Livorno.

This picture was commissioned in 1787 by the Comte d'Angiviller, Directeur-Général des Bâtiments du Roi, as a pendant to a picture he already owned, a smaller version by Jacques-Louis David of his great *Belisarius*, the larger version of which is now in the Musée des Beaux-Arts, Lille. Gauffier's painting depicts the meeting of Cleopatra and Octavian as described in Charles Rollin's *Histoire Romaine...*, first published in 1730–38 and based on Plutarch's *Lives*. After he defeated the forces of Antony at the battle of Actium (31 BC) Octavian visited Cleopatra who, seductively but unsuccessfuly, attempted to convince him of her innocence and remorse for the part she played in opposing him. Unmoved, Octavian rejected all her excuses whereupon Cleopatra directed his attention to his great-uncle Julius Caesar, reading from the tender letters she had received from him and pointing out the portraits of Caesar which were displayed in her room.

Cleopatra and Octavian is a fascinating example of the vogue for Egyptian art and motifs, known as Egyptomania, which swept France and Britain in the late eighteenth and early nineteenth centuries and was promulgated by figures such as Thomas Hope (1769–1831), the collector, patron and writer. Intriguingly, the throne in Gauffier's painting was copied exactly by Hope for four seats in his London house at Duchess Street and he later became one of Gauffier's major patrons, owning five paintings by him.

Gauffier's work has only recently been acknowledged by a wider public. When this picture was exported from France in the 1980s it bore a false signature indicating it was by J.-L. David! There is a small preparatory oil sketch for the composition, now in a French private collection, which has borne various attributions to David and J.-B. Mallet, but which is now generally acknowledged to be by Gauffier.

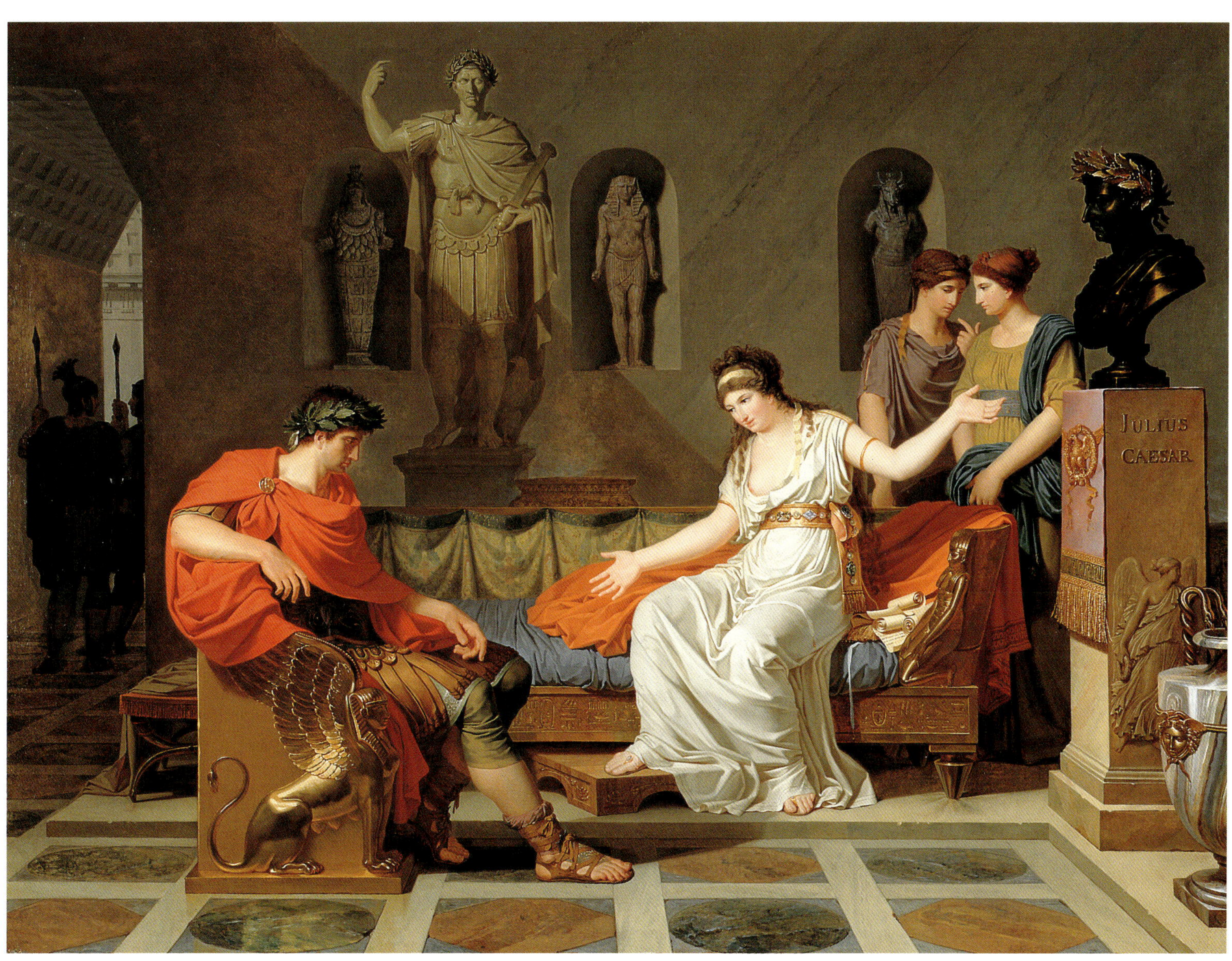
JULIUS
CAESAR

Jean-Victor Bertin 1767–1842

30 *Classical Landscape*, 1800

Oil on canvas · 25 × 34¼in (63.5 × 87cm)
Signed and dated, lower right: Bertin/an VIII [1800]
Purchased 1988
NG 2465

A pupil of the father of neoclassical landscape painting, Pierre-Henri de Valenciennes (1750–1819), Bertin was a regular exhibitor at the Paris Salon from 1793 until his death. A number of his works were purchased by the State and placed in official residences such as Trianon and Fontainebleau. He was highly instrumental in the establishment in 1816 of a competition held every four years for the Prix de Rome for Historical Landscape Painting: this marked a significant step in the emancipation of landscape painting as a separate category in French art. Bertin ran a studio which was of considerable importance for the history of landscape painting in France and his many talented pupils included Coignet, Fleury, Boisselier, Roqueplan and Corot (formerly a pupil of Michallon, Corot was distinctly uncomplimentary about Bertin's capabilities).

Classical Landscape is a typical, highly finished landscape of the period, greatly influenced by the example of seventeenth-century landscape painters such as Claude Lorrain and Nicolas Poussin. Neoclassical landscape presented nature in idealised form, as it ought to be rather than as it was, recalling the world of classical antiquity which inspired such visions. Recently there has been an upsurge of interest in such painting, particularly in the preparatory oil-sketches which the neoclassical masters executed in the open air in preparation for their finished studio landscapes such as this one. The freshness and spontaneity of many of these sketches has led many commentators to claim them as the forerunners of Impressionism. In the process the often very considerable merits of finished landscapes such as *Classical Landscape* have been unjustly overlooked.

This is one of Bertin's finest pictures and was probably shown by him at the 1800 Salon in Paris. Its details match the contemporary descriptions of exhibit no.21 *Deux bergers offrent un sacrifice au dieu Pan* ('Two shepherds offer a sacrifice to the god Pan'). However, the measurements given in the Salon catalogue accord with those of the picture frame rather than the painting itself. It is highly likely that the frame measurements were recorded by mistake and that the present frame is, in fact, the picture's original one.

Bertin had already depicted a landscape with an offering to Pan in 1796, and the subject recurs again in a large painting he exhibited at the 1817 Salon, to critical praise, and which was placed on deposit in the Musée des Beaux-Arts in Rennes in 1824.

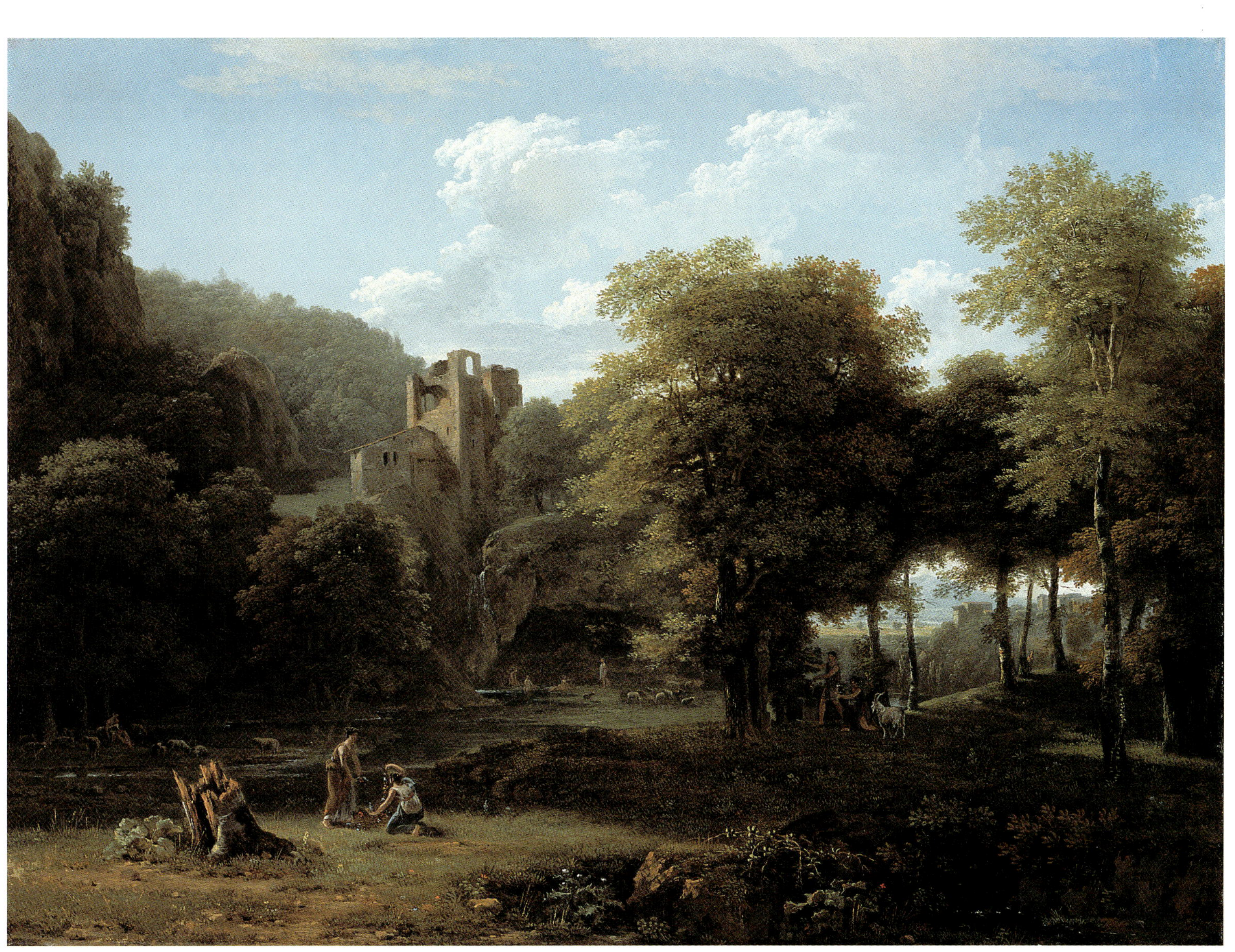

François, Baron Gérard 1770–1837

31 *Madame Mère*, *c*.1800–4

Oil on canvas · 82¾ × 51⅛in (210.8 × 129.8cm)
Inscribed, lower left: Fco Gerard.
Purchased with the aid of the National Art Collections Fund 1988
NG 2461

Gérard became the leading portraitist of the Napoleonic era in France and was also well patronised after the Restoration of the monarchy under the Bourbons, being created baron in 1819. He was born in Rome where his father worked for the household of Cardinal de Bernis, French ambassador to the Papal States. His family returned to France in 1780 and Gérard studied with the sculptor Pajou and then with the painter Brenet before entering the studio of Jacques-Louis David in 1786. His reputation was established with his *Portrait of Isabey* (Louvre, Paris), shown at the 1796 Salon, and his *Cupid and Psyche* (Louvre, Paris) of 1798. He also enjoyed great success as a history painter during both the Empire and the Restoration.

This imposingly formal portrait of Napoleon's mother probably dates from 1800 to 1804, the period during which Napoleon was Consul – the portrait bust in the background depicts him in this role. Maria Laetitia Ramolino Bonaparte (1750–1836) was born in Ajaccio, Corsica, to a family of Tuscan origin, and married in 1764 Charles-Marie Bonaparte, a lawyer who had trained in Pisa. He died in 1786. They had thirteen children of whom eight survived and the second eldest was Napoleon. In 1805, shortly after his coronation as Emperor, Napoleon conferred on his mother the title 'Son Altesse impériale Madame, mère de l'Empereur' and she was known thenceforth as 'Madame Mère'. She is depicted seated in a matron-like pose ultimately derived from the fourth-century sculpture known as the *Seated Agrippina* (Capitoline Museum, Rome) and with a view through to the Tuileries beyond. Faced with such a hieratic image of imperial matriarchy it is easy to forget that the sitter could barely write and only spoke French with difficulty in a strong Corsican accent.

There are two closely related autograph seated portraits of Madame Mère, one shows her with a statue of Fecunditas (doubtless intended as a reference to the size of her family) and is in a French private collection, the other is now at the Château de Malmaison and features a laureate bust of Napoleon, indicative of his status as Emperor.

The Edinburgh version enjoyed a somewhat chequered history. It was probably given by Napoleon to his younger brother Jérôme, King of Westphalia 1807–13, who would have hung it at his palace at Kassel. Jérôme's later financial problems caused him in 1840 to marry off his daughter Mathilde to Anatole, one of the spectacularly rich Demidoff family, and the picture may well have formed part of her dowry. After being exhibited 1851–9 by Anatole at the Napoleonic Musée de San Martino on the island of Elba, it was removed by his son Paul to the family's Villa of San Donato, just outside Florence, where it hung near a copy of Canova's great seated sculpture of Madame Mère, the original of which is now at Chatsworth House, Derbyshire.

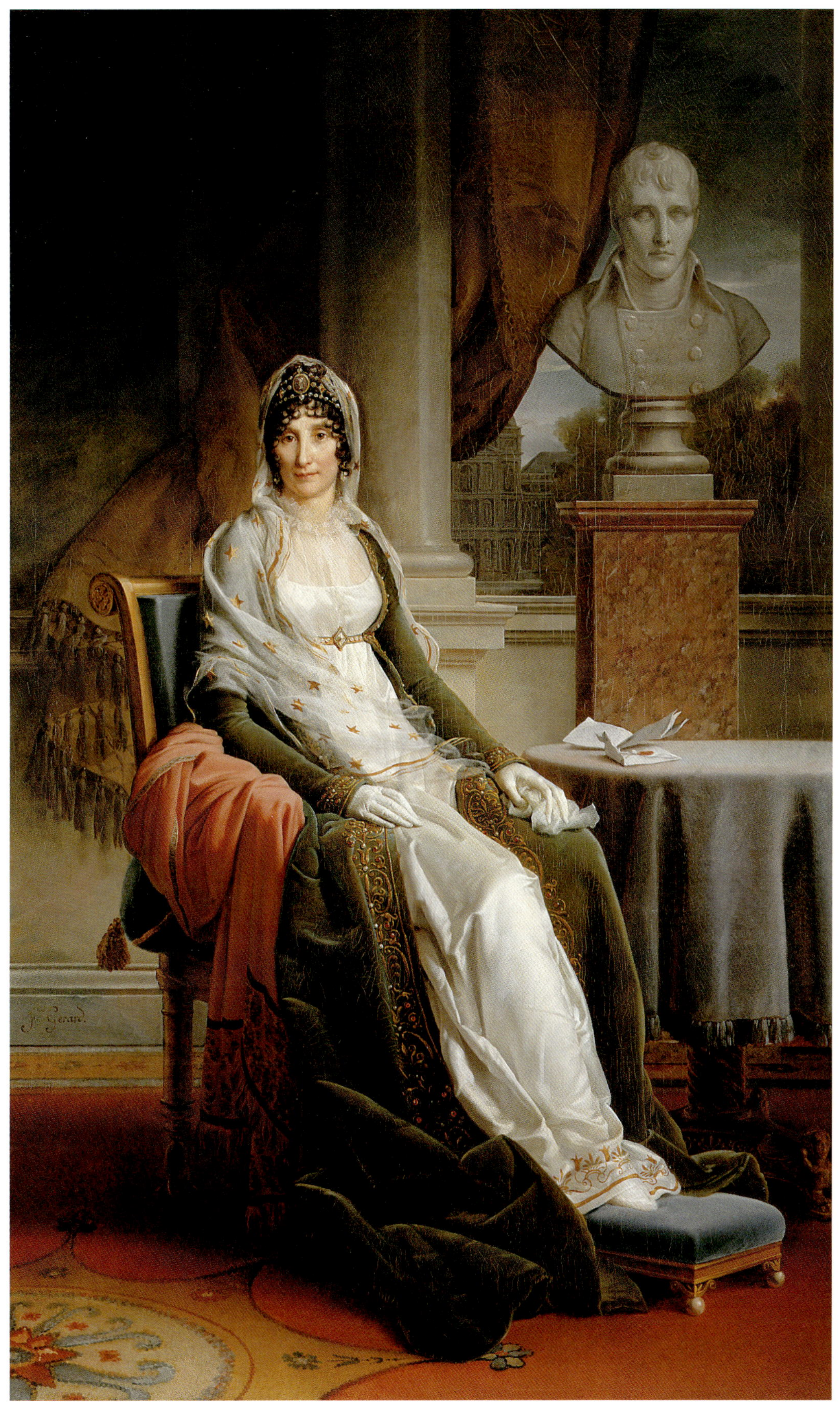

Eugène Delacroix 1798–1863

32 *Arabs Playing Chess, c.1847–8*

Oil on canvas · 18⅛ × 21⅞in (46 × 55cm)
Signed, lower left: Eug.Delacroix
Purchased 1957
NG 2190

The leading painter of the Romantic movement in France, Delacroix was born at Charenton-Saint-Maurice, the fourth child of Charles Delacroix, ambassador plenipotentiary to the Netherlands, and Victoire Oeben, daughter of the renowned cabinetmaker to Louis XV. Although brought up in difficult circumstances, he received an excellent education and, as a child, was a frequent visitor to the Louvre where he was able to view the great collection of masterpieces which Napoleon had amassed from around Europe. Delacroix studied under the painter Pierre-Narcisse Guérin and also worked for a short time at the Ecole des Beaux-Arts in Paris. He visited London in 1825, and in 1832 accompanied the diplomatic mission to Spain headed by the Comte de Mornay. His enormous painting *The Massacre of Chios* (Louvre, Paris), exhibited at the Salon in 1824, confirmed his position at the head of the Romantic movement. Delacroix's use of broken areas of colour in this picture was of considerable importance for future artists, notably the Impressionists. An immensely prolific artist, Delacroix left a fascinating account of his life and art in his *Journal*.

Near Eastern and North African subjects appealed particularly to Romantic painters and writers; they were considered to stimulate both the senses and the imagination, and they were also associated with the unknown and the exotic. The scene depicted here was doubtless based on Delacroix's recollections of his North African trip of 1832 and may refer to similar scenes he witnessed in Meknes and Oran. The picture has been dated by Lee Johnson to 1847–8 (*The Paintings of Eugène Delacroix. A Critical Catalogue*, III, Oxford, 1986, no.379, pl.187). Its exact title is problematical, however. In his *Journal* Delacroix recorded working at Champrosay in 1847 on *Arabes jouant aux echécs*, presumably this painting. However, it was reproduced in an aquatint by Ferdinand Lefman in *L'Artiste* (of which the picture's first owner, Arsène Houssaye, was editor) for 1 March 1848 with the title *Jouers d'échecs à Jerusalem*. The published commentary also gave a biblical identification for the water-carrier as 'Rebecca returning from the Well' (Genesis 24).

The chronicle of the picture's ownership reveals its changing fortunes. Houssaye probably gave it back to the artist, who in turn sold it to the dealer, Weill, in 1849. Its later owners included the dealer Durand-Ruel, who played such a crucial role in the promotion of Impressionism, and the Art Institute of Chicago, which purchased it in 1900 but then disposed of it in 1931.

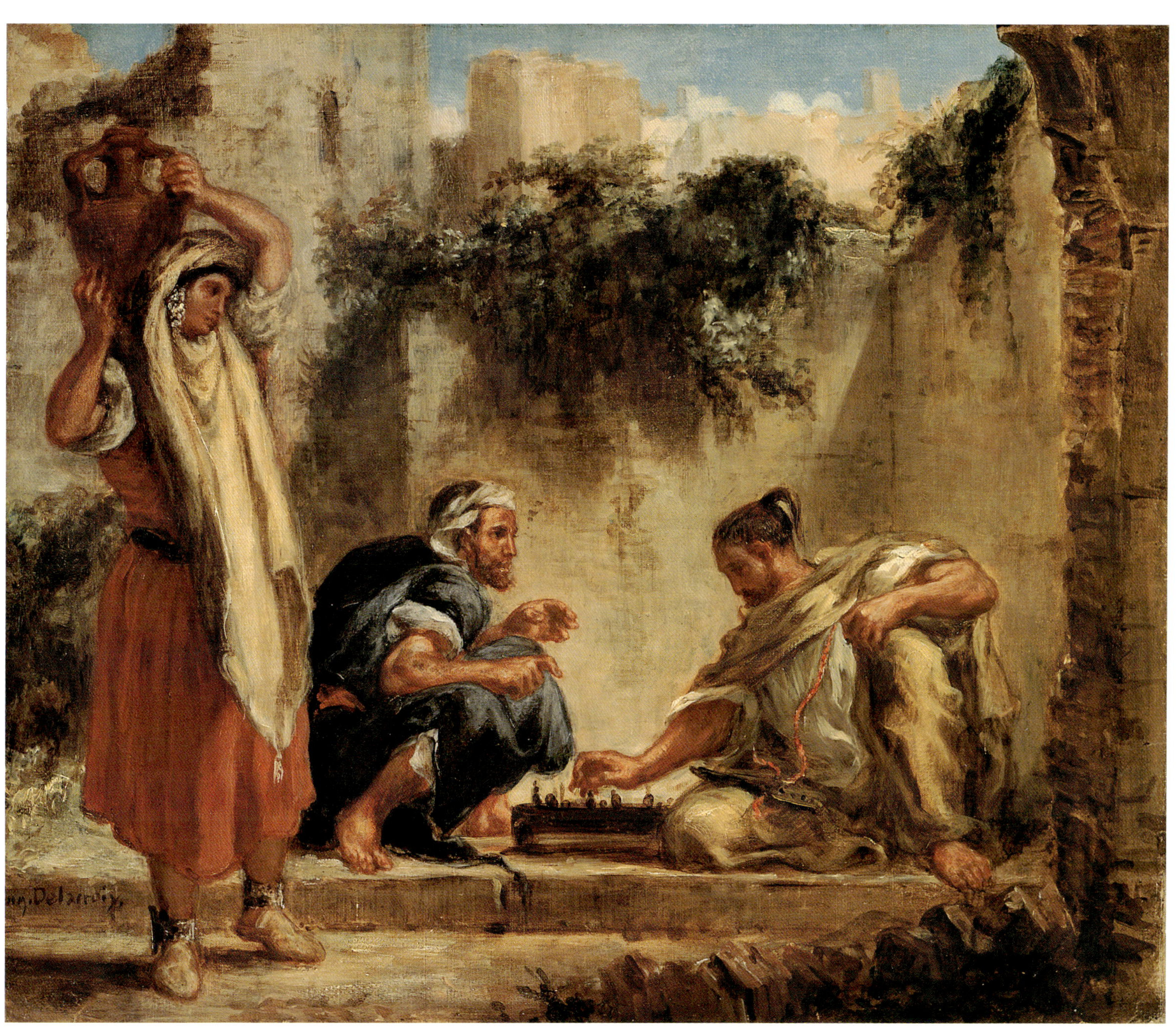

Angelica Kauffman 1741–1807

33 *Michael Novosielski*, 1791

Oil on canvas · 50½ × 40in (128 × 101.6cm)
Signed and dated: *Angelica Kauffman / Pinxt. Roma 1791*
Bequest of Mrs Elizabeth Stewart 1879
NG 651

Angelica Kauffman was born at Coire, Switzerland, the daughter of the painter Joseph Johann Kauffman who taught her music and painting from an early age. She was undoubtedly one of the best known and most successful women artists of the eighteenth century. Chaperoned by her father, she trained in Italy from 1754 to 1757, and again from 1762 to 1766. She secured membership of three Italian fine art academies and was associated with several of the leading exponents of neoclassical style in Rome. Kauffman then came to England where she became one of only two women elected as founder members of the elitist and male-dominated Royal Academy. The annual exhibitions held there, at which she exhibited 1769–97, also encouraged her sustained experimentation with grand history painting whose principal theoretician, Sir Joshua Reynolds, was a rejected suitor of Angelica's.

While society portraiture remained the most lucrative branch of her career, Angelica also carried out decorative wall and ceiling paintings in many English and a few Irish houses, matching perfectly the interiors created by the neoclassical architect Robert Adam (1728–1792). Some of these decorative schemes were carried out in collaboration with a Venetian artist working in Britain, Antonio Zucchi (1726–1795), whom she married in 1781. Following this, she moved to Italy, where she attracted an international clientele and her portraits enjoyed virtually unrivalled status, following the death of Pompeo Batoni in 1787. She also instigated a Salon that became a forum for high society, frequented by the writer Goethe and the sculptor Antonio Canova, the latter of whom was later to plan Kauffman's funeral in direct emulation of the ceremony held at Raphael's death.

The sitter for this portrait was the architect Michael Novosielski (1750–1795), the son of the Polish refugee Count Novosielski. Michael was born in Rome but later settled in England in about 1770, to help James Wyatt with the building of the Pantheon (1770–2). He was also a contemporary and friend of the architect Sir John Soane. Novosielski is shown here holding a plan of his design for the rebuilding in 1790–1 of London's Haymarket Opera House (following a fire of 27 June 1789), also known as the King's Theatre (see Lady V. Manners and G.C. Williamson, *Angelica Kauffmann RA: Her Life and her Works*, London, 1924, cat.no.26, and *Hommage an Angelica Kauffmann*, exhibition catalogue, Liechtensteinische Staatliche Kunstsammlung, Vaduz, and Palazzo della Permanente, Milan, 1992–3, cat.no.56). Apart from La Scala in Milan, it was then the largest theatre in Europe but was destroyed by fire in 1867, a perennial theatrical hazard, and is now the site of Her Majesty's Theatre, Haymarket. The plan clearly shows a 'horseshoe' shaped auditorium, a design that Novosielski introduced to Britain from theatre layouts he knew from Italy and Bordeaux. Novosielski lived with his wife, the Countess Felicia Regina, at Michael's Place, Brompton, London, which he had built as a speculation, along with Michael's Grove and Brompton Crescent (which were all pulled down for redevelopment in 1886). They had four children, one of whom, Michael Peter, bequeathed this painting of his father to his wife, Elizabeth (later Mrs Stewart), who left the portrait to the National Gallery of Scotland at her husband's behest.

Kauffman also painted a companion portrait of Count Novosielski's wife, Felicia Regina, which shows her wearing a white dress and dark shawl, a workbasket upon her lap, set against a wooded landscape (Donnington Priory Salerooms, 5 April, 2000, lot 104, repr.). Both canvases are dated 1791 and were painted in Rome. According to the memorandum notebook of Angelica's husband, however, it appears that the pictures, which cost 120 *zecchini* (Roman sequins) each, were not actually completed until March the following year. They were then dispatched to the British expatriate dealer and antiquary in Rome, Thomas Jenkins, who took charge of shipping them back to Britain. (Jenkins later lost money by investing in one of Novosielski's speculative building schemes in Sidmouth, curtailed by the architect's death.) It is not known how long the Novosielskis spent on their visit to Rome in 1791 but presumably it was a chance to catch up on old friends and family there.

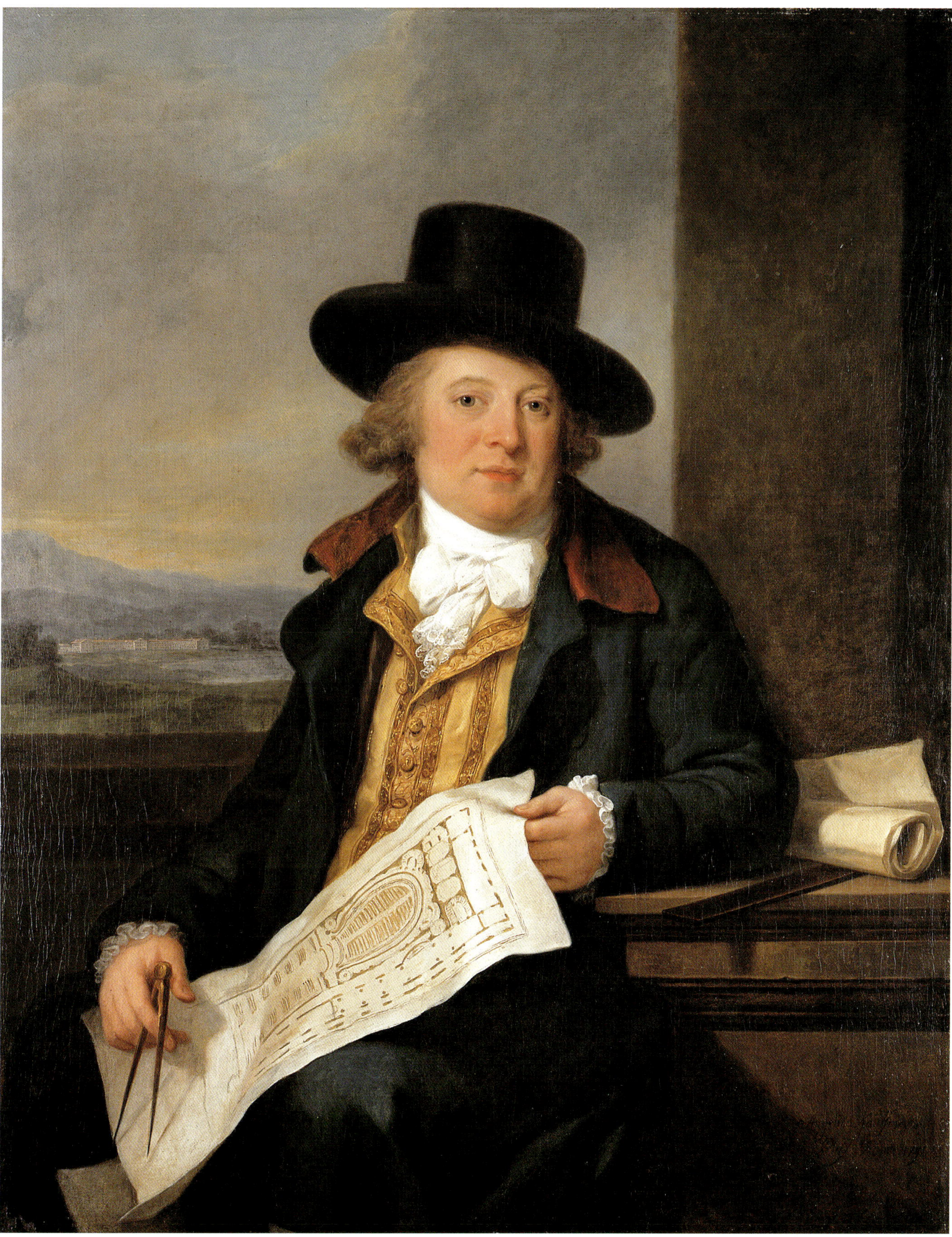

Allan Ramsay 1713–1784

34 *Mary Digges, Lady Robert Manners*, 1760s

Oil on canvas · 29¼ × 24¼in (74.3 × 61.6cm) (oval)
Bequest of Mrs Nisbet Hamilton Ogilvy of Biel 1921
NG 1523

In 1756 Mary Digges (1737–1829), the only daughter and heiress of Colonel Thomas Digges of Roehampton in Surrey, married Lord Robert Manners, eighth son of the 2nd Duke of Rutland. Through this alliance she became associated with a dynasty whose sustained patronage of Allan Ramsay over two generations had been initiated during the inaugural phase of the artist's career in London and which she herself was to perpetuate by sitting for her own portrait during the late 1760s. The Manners family patronage of Ramsay appears to have originated with her future sister-in-law, Lady Lucy Manners, later Duchess of Montrose, whose modest half-length portrait of 1739 is also in the National Gallery of Scotland's collection. A year later, Lord Sherard Manners, the sixth son of the 2nd Duke of Rutland, followed his sister's example and in 1745 the distinguished General John Manners, Marquess of Granby, eldest son of the 3rd Duke and subsequently nephew by marriage of Lady Robert Manners, commissioned a new full-length portrait now in the custody of English Heritage at Audley End in Essex (see, A. Smart (ed. J. Ingamells), *Allan Ramsay: A Complete Catalogue of His Paintings*, New Haven and London, 1999, cat.nos.204, 351–2 and 372).

In 1921, through the bequest of the lineal descendant of the Ladies Lucy and Mary Manners, the Ramsay portraits of the two sisters-in-law were reunited within the Gallery's collection where they provide a fascinating illustration of the artist's development between the late 1730s and the late 1760s. The eldest son and namesake of Allan Ramsay, the poet and author of *The Gentle Shepherd*, the younger Ramsay enrolled at the Academy of St Luke in Edinburgh in 1729. After seeking further instruction from the Swedish portrait painter Hans Hysing in London, he established an independent portrait practice in Edinburgh in 1732. From 1736 successive extended formative visits to Italy, where he initially studied with Imperiali and Solimena, accelerated Ramsay's transformation into a portraitist of European stature and sophistication. By the close of the year 1738, when Ramsay settled permanently in London, the Scottish antiquary Alexander Gordon was able to report that, with the possible exception of his London-based Italian contemporary Andrea Soldi, Ramsay had no equal among portrait painters in Great Britain. It was this rising reputation which evidently drew Lady Lucy Manners to his Covent Garden studio in 1739 for a portrait whose indebtedness to the inherited conventions of indigenous British portraiture was still strikingly predominant. Over two decades later, following Ramsay's second visit to Italy (1754–7), Lady Mary Manners was to benefit from the artist's lifelong quest for a more natural and informal mode of presentation in an exquisite application of his mature style in female portraiture.

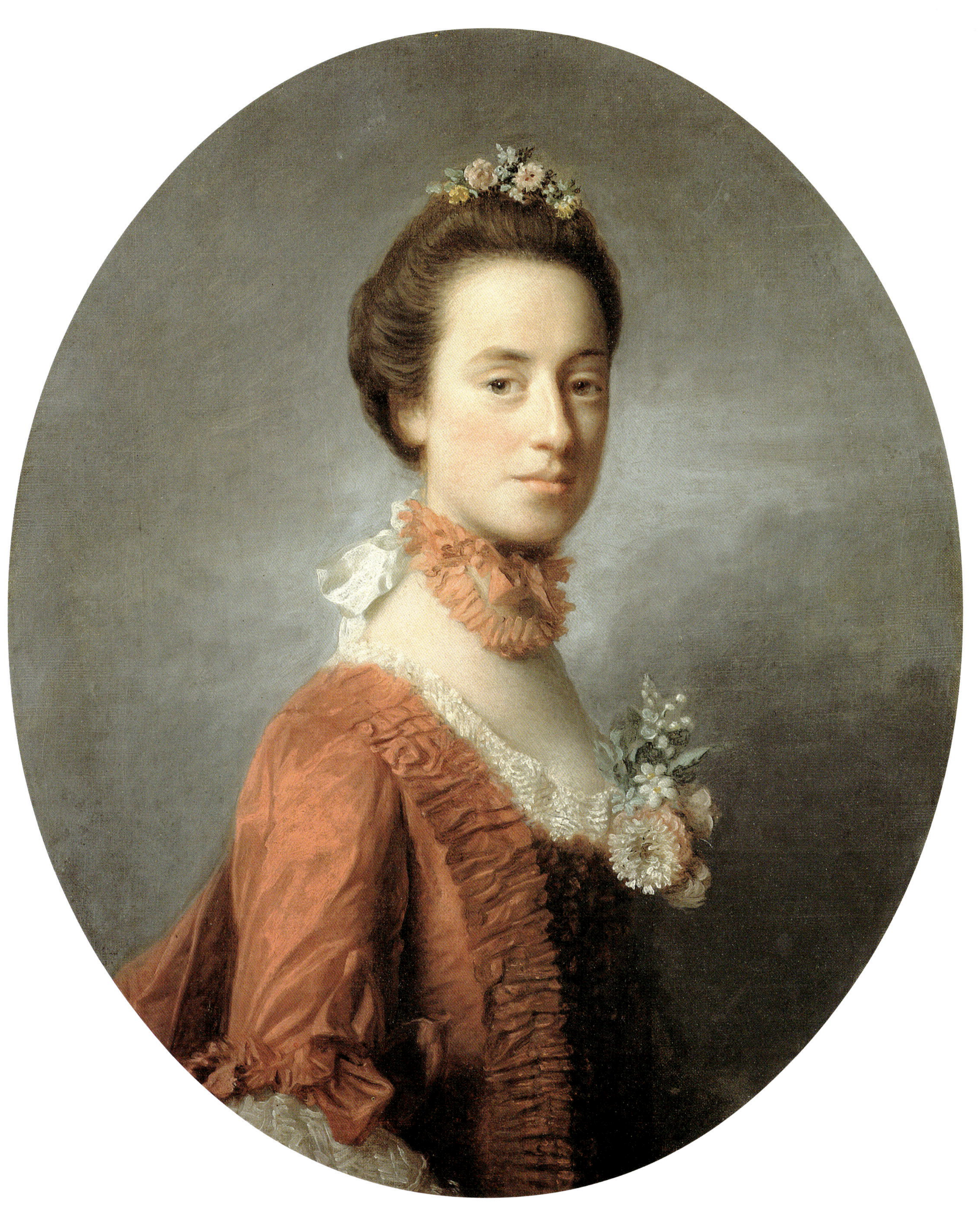

Jacob More 1740–1793

35 *Mount Vesuvius in Eruption ('The Last Days of Pompeii')*, 1780

Oil on canvas · 59½ × 79in (151 × 201cm)
Inscribed, signed and dated towards the centre: Jacob More / Rome / 1780
Presented to the Royal Institution for the Encouragement of the Fine Arts in Scotland by Sir John James Steuart of Allanbank 1829; transferred to the National Gallery of Scotland 1859
NG 290

In 1767 More's stage scenery for the New Theatre in Edinburgh was so favourably received that he determined to specialise in landscape exclusively. That same year his former master Alexander Runciman, who had trained in the Scottish tradition of decorative painting developed by the Norie family, left for Italy, thus affording More an opportunity to dominate the practice of landscape painting in Scotland. The 1771 London exhibition of the first set of his views of the three 'sublime and terrible' falls on the River Clyde in Lanarkshire transformed him into one of Britain's leading landscape painters who also enjoyed celebrity status in his native Edinburgh. At the exhibition of the Incorporated Society of Artists in 1771 his *Falls of Clyde (Cora Linn)*, now in the Gallery's collection, was purchased by Reynolds who considered More 'the best painter of air since Claude'. From the winter of 1771/2 More settled permanently in Italy where, as a prominent member of the expatriate Scots community, he became known internationally as 'More of Rome' and the outstanding British neoclassical painter of his time. In 1775 he accompanied his compatriot Allan Ramsay as a draughtsman during the latter's search for Horace's Sabine Villa near Licenza. During the following decade More was engaged on the sumptuous re-decoration of the room in the Villa Borghese in Rome which accommodated Bernini's great sculptural group *Apollo and Daphne*. More's final commission for the Prince Borghese was the creation of the Giardino Inglese in the Borghese gardens (see J. Holloway, *Jacob More 1740–1793*, Edinburgh, 1987).

In 1780 Antonio Canova admired in More's Roman studio a brilliantly theatrical representation of Mount Vesuvius, worked up from 'flying sketches' executed at night during the most recent eruption in 1779. The sculptor observed that More had conceived the spectacle 'come descrive plinio' ('as described by Pliny') and therefore as a history painting rather than as a pure landscape. In the middle distance the city of Pompeii is on fire while in the foreground, among the fleeing figures in classical dress, Pliny the Elder is shown dying during the eruption of AD 79, the whole catastrophe being vividly described in the correspondence of his nephew Pliny the Younger. More's *Vesuvius* may correspond to the painting celebrating fire in a set dedicated to the four elements which was commissioned by Lord Bristol, the Earl-Bishop of Derry, one of More's most committed patrons and a keen amateur vulcanologist (see D. Irwin, 'Jacob More, Neo-Classical Landscape Painter', *Burlington Magazine*, vol.CXIV, May 1972, pp.777–8; P. R. Andrew, 'Jacob More and the Earl-Bishop of Derry', *Apollo*, August 1986, pp.88–94; and P. R. Andrew, 'Jacob More: Biography and a Checklist of Works', *The Walpole Society*, vol.LV, pp.105–96 and cat.no.B.18.ii).

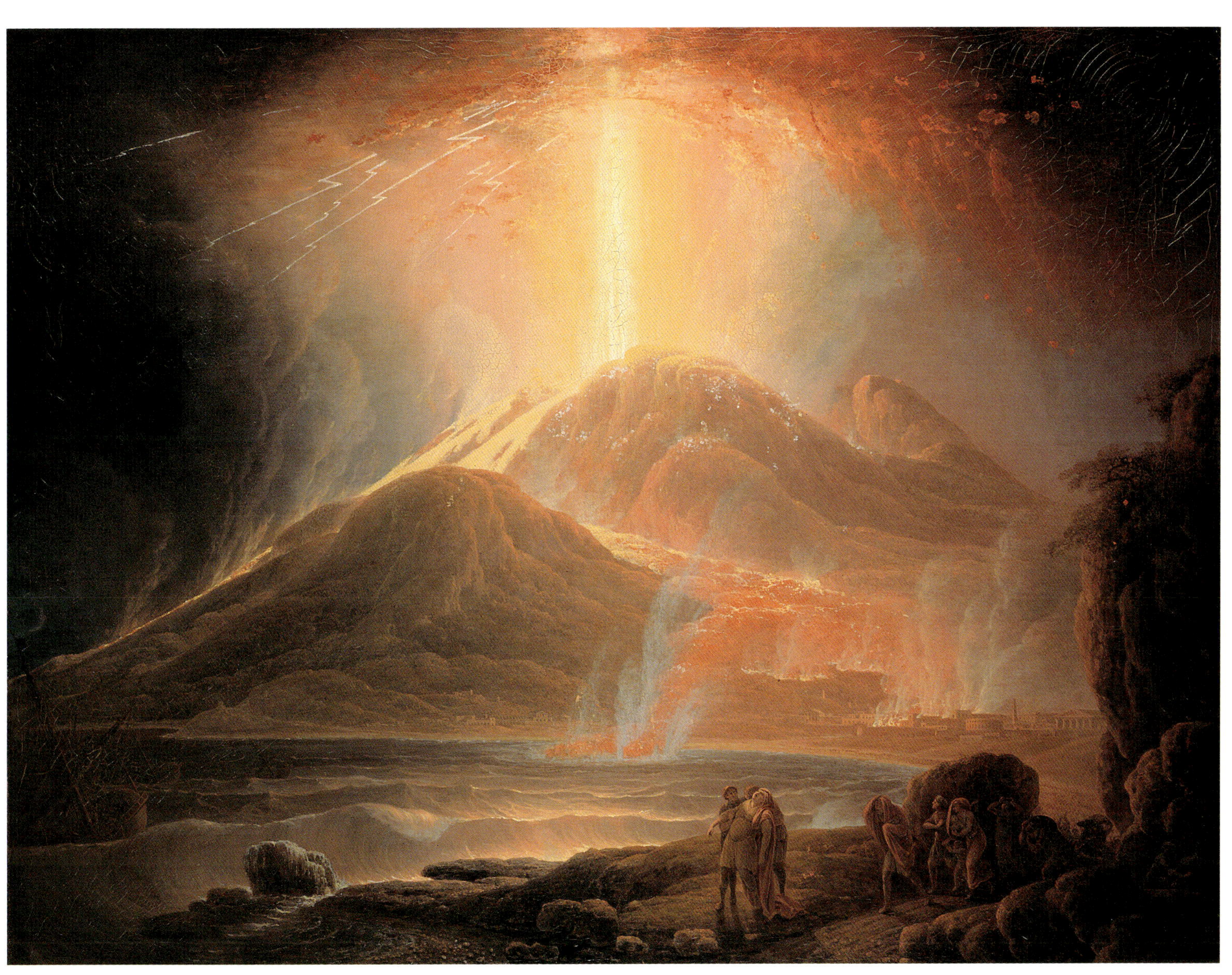

Sir David Wilkie 1785–1841

36 *William Chalmers Bethune, his second wife Isobel Morison and their daughter Isabella Maxwell Morison*, 1804

Oil on canvas · 49½ × 40½in (125.7 × 102.9cm)
Signed and dated bottom left: D. Wilkie/1804
Purchased with the Barrogill Keith Bequest Fund, with additional funding from the Rutherford and Laird McDougall Funds and the Cowan Smith Bequest Fund 1985
NG 2433

In 1799 the precociously gifted fourteen-year-old Wilkie, son of the parish minister of Cults in Fife, entered the Trustees' Academy in Edinburgh where his fellow students included John Burnet, subsequently Wilkie's memorialist and principal engraver. By 1802 the drawing academy's elementary curriculum had been restructured to incorporate oil painting and a system of annual premiums for the best historical composition. Two years later Wilkie embarked on his first major subject picture, a complex vernacular narrative 'portrait' of the annual May fair which took place in Pitlessie village in the vicinity of his native Cults. The painting of *Pitlessie Fair* (National Gallery of Scotland), a radical and ultimately extremely influential departure from the prescribed conventions of history painting in the grand manner, was to establish the fundamental orientation of his later career.

Wilkie's celebratory 'portrait' of his local fair was commissioned by Thomas Kinnear of Kinloch, a neighbour of William Chalmers of Pittmeddan near Auchtermuchty whose family were to award the Fifeshire prodigy two ambitious portrait commissions in 1804 and 1805 successively. A lawyer by profession and clerk to the Chancery in Scotland of the Prince of Wales, Chalmers (1744–1807) had first married and assumed the surname of Margaret Bethune, an heiress from Blebo near St Andrews. His second marriage to Isobel Morison (1760–1850) of Naughton House in the locality of Wormit produced his only child and heiress, Isabella (1795–1818), who was to sit for the second time to Wilkie in 1805 with her maternal grandfather, James Morison, for a conversation piece in the manner of Raeburn (sold at Sothebys, London, 6 April 1993, lot 60). Following the premature death of Isabella, her mother bequeathed the estate of Naughton to a distant relative Adam Morison Duncan, the great-grandson of Viscount Duncan, victor of the Battle of Camperdown, in the possession of whose descendants Wilkie's monumental triple portrait remained until its acquisition by the Gallery in 1985 (for Wilkie's early Fifeshire patronage, see Allan Cunningham, *Sir David Wilkie*, London, 1843, I, p.67 and the catalogue (by H.A.D. Miles and D. Blayney Brown) of the exhibition, *Sir David Wilkie of Scotland (1785–1841)*, North Carolina Museum of Art, Raleigh, 1987, cat.nos.2 and 4).

In May 1805 Wilkie made his decisive move to London and the Royal Academy Schools with their superior facilities for art education. He carried with him, as his showpiece and prospectus, *Pitlessie Fair* which was seen by the Earl of Mansfield. The following year the exhibition of *The Village Politicians*, painted for Lord Mansfield and now displayed at Scone Palace near Perth, drew prodigious crowds at the Royal Academy and elicited a commission for *The Blind Fiddler* (Tate, London) from Sir George Beaumont. In 1805, at the exceptionally young age of twenty-four and having exhibited only five paintings in London, Wilkie was elected an Associate of the Royal Academy. The committed patronage of Chalmers Bethune and his fellow Fifeshire landowners had served him well.

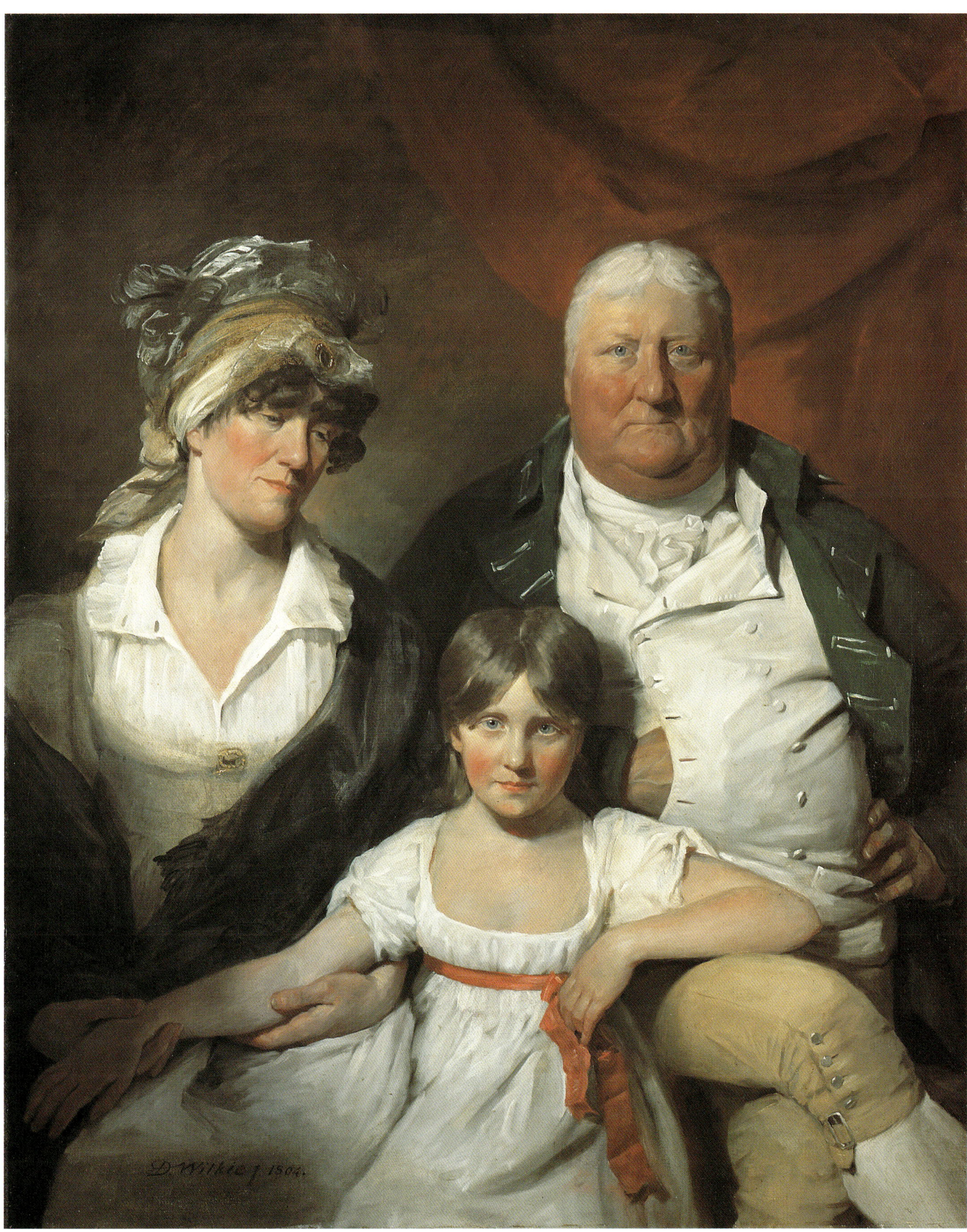
D. Wilkie f. 1804.

Sir Henry Raeburn 1756–1823

37 *Colonel Alastair Ranaldson Macdonell of Glengarry*, exhibited 1812

Oil on canvas · 95 × 59in (241 × 150cm)
Purchased 1917
NG 420

The death of Raeburn's former mentor David Martin in 1797 consolidated the younger artist's position as the doyen of portrait painters in the Scottish capital and, by extension, in the whole of Scotland. In the course of 1798, Raeburn's expanding business obliged him to move to a more capacious, custom-designed studio at 16 York Place, Edinburgh, which has been preserved in essentials to the present day (now renumbered 32). On 2 March 1810, immediately after the death of the London-based portrait painter John Hoppner, David Wilkie noted in his private journal that, despite Raeburn's localised success, he was intending to take the lease of Hoppner's house with a view to settling permanently in London. That June Wilkie accompanied his compatriot to the Crown and Anchor where he was fêted by members of the Royal Academy including the President, Benjamin West.

Although Raeburn's experimentation with the London market proved abortive, he continued to harbour an ambition for formalised recognition by the Royal Academy and to court the attention of English patrons by contributing annually to the Academy's exhibitions from 1810 until 1823. That ambition was to be fulfilled partially in 1812 by his election as an Associate and completely in 1814 by his admission to the full status of Academician. Raeburn's principal contribution in 1812 was the *Portrait of the Chief of the Macdonells* which was presumably completed shortly before the Royal Academy exhibition.

The proscription on the wearing of Highland dress which followed the 'Forty-Five' [1745] Jacobite Rising had been lifted in 1782. Macdonell may well have wished to emulate, in changed times and with romantic panache, the flamboyant public image of Highland chieftainship which Raeburn had already so memorably portrayed in the late 1790s in his great full-length of Sir John Sinclair of Ulbster, also in the Gallery's collection (see D. Thomson *et al*, *Raeburn. The Art of Sir Henry Raeburn 1756–1823*, exhibition catalogue, National Galleries of Scotland, Edinburgh, 1987, cat.nos.28 and 47). Sir Walter Scott's pen portrait of Macdonell of Glengarry (1771–1828) captured to perfection the anachronistic and idiosyncratic lifestyle of his close friend and contemporary on whom he probably based the character of the doomed Jacobite clan chieftain Fergus McIvor in his novel *Waverley*: 'This gentleman is a kind of Quixote in our age, having retaind in its full extent whole feelings of Clanship and Chieftainship elsewhere so long abandoned. He seems to have lived a century too late and to exist in a state of complete law and order like a Glengarry of old whose will was law to his sept.' Yet, despite his passion for the customs and social structures of Gaelic culture of the era prior to the Forty-Five Rising, Macdonell evicted his tenants to clear the land for sheep farming. His life ended with appropriate high drama when he leapt from the canal steamer *Stirling Castle* as it was grounded in Loch Linnhe. His passing was mourned by Scott at the Celtic Society's dinner in Edinburgh in January 1828.

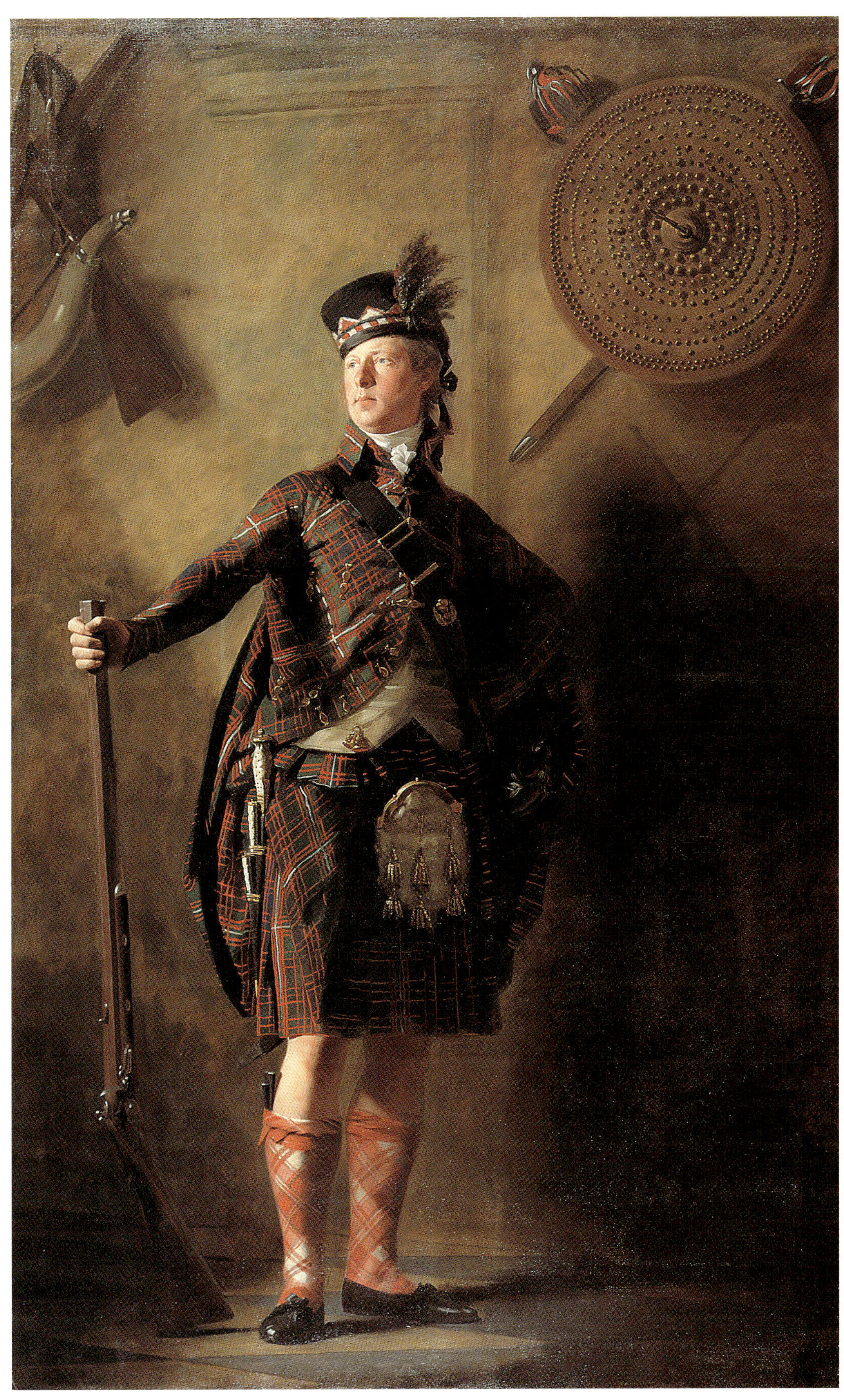

Alexander Nasmyth 1758–1840

38 *Princes Street with the Commencement of the Building of the Royal Institution*, 1825

Oil on canvas · 48¼ × 65in (122.5 × 165.5cm)
Inscribed, signed and dated bottom right: A. Nasmyth/Edinburgh/1825
Presented by Sir David Baird 1991
NG 2542

This spectacular view of Edinburgh is a particularly impressive example of the mature work of Nasmyth whom Wilkie honoured as the 'founder of the landscape painting school of Scotland.' The son of an Edinburgh master-builder, Nasmyth studied drawing at the Trustees' Academy under Alexander Runciman, while concurrently serving an apprenticeship with a local house-painter. In their turn, both of Nasmyth's masters had trained with the Norie family, the leading firm of house-painters which had pioneered the art of pure as well as applied landscape painting in Scotland. In 1774 Nasmyth was engaged by Allan Ramsay as a specialist drapery painter in his London studio before establishing his own successful portrait practice in Edinburgh. During the 1790s Nasmyth evolved his most influential type of landscape painting – large-scale panoramic views of Scottish country houses and castles in which topographical accuracy was united with a distinctive picturesque sensibility. Nasmyth's manner was widely disseminated through his classes for amateur and intending professional artists which convened at his custom-built premises at 47 York Place in Edinburgh and for which his daughters, all of whom achieved some independent recognition as landscape painters, provided collaborative instruction.

Nasmyth's panorama records both the city itself and its burgeoning cultural life at a dramatic stage of transition (see J. C. B. Cooksey, *Alexander Nasmyth HRSA, 1758–1840: A Man of the Scottish Renaissance*, Haddington, 1991, cat.no.021). From a vantage point at the junction of Hanover Street and Princes Street, the artist's outlook encompasses both the late mediaeval Old Town and the neoclassical New Town with a vista towards Arthur's Seat and the Nelson Monument on Calton Hill. On the right, emerging from a building site on the artificial earthen mound which linked the Old with the New Town, is the Doric temple to the arts commissioned from William Henry Playfair, one of the principal architects of the New Town, and opened in 1826. (Playfair himself may well be the figure addressing the masons in the right foreground of the picture, dressed in a black frock coat and hat). Now known as the Royal Scottish Academy building, Playfair's multi-purpose Doric temple originally served as the venue for the pioneering exhibitions of Old Master and contemporary Scottish painting staged by the Institution for the Encouragement of the Fine Arts in Scotland. In addition, the building provided improved accommodation for the Trustees' Academy and ultimately for the Scottish Academy formed in 1826 and incorporated by royal charter in 1838. Playfair later designed the adjacent National Gallery of Scotland of which the foundation stone was laid in 1850.

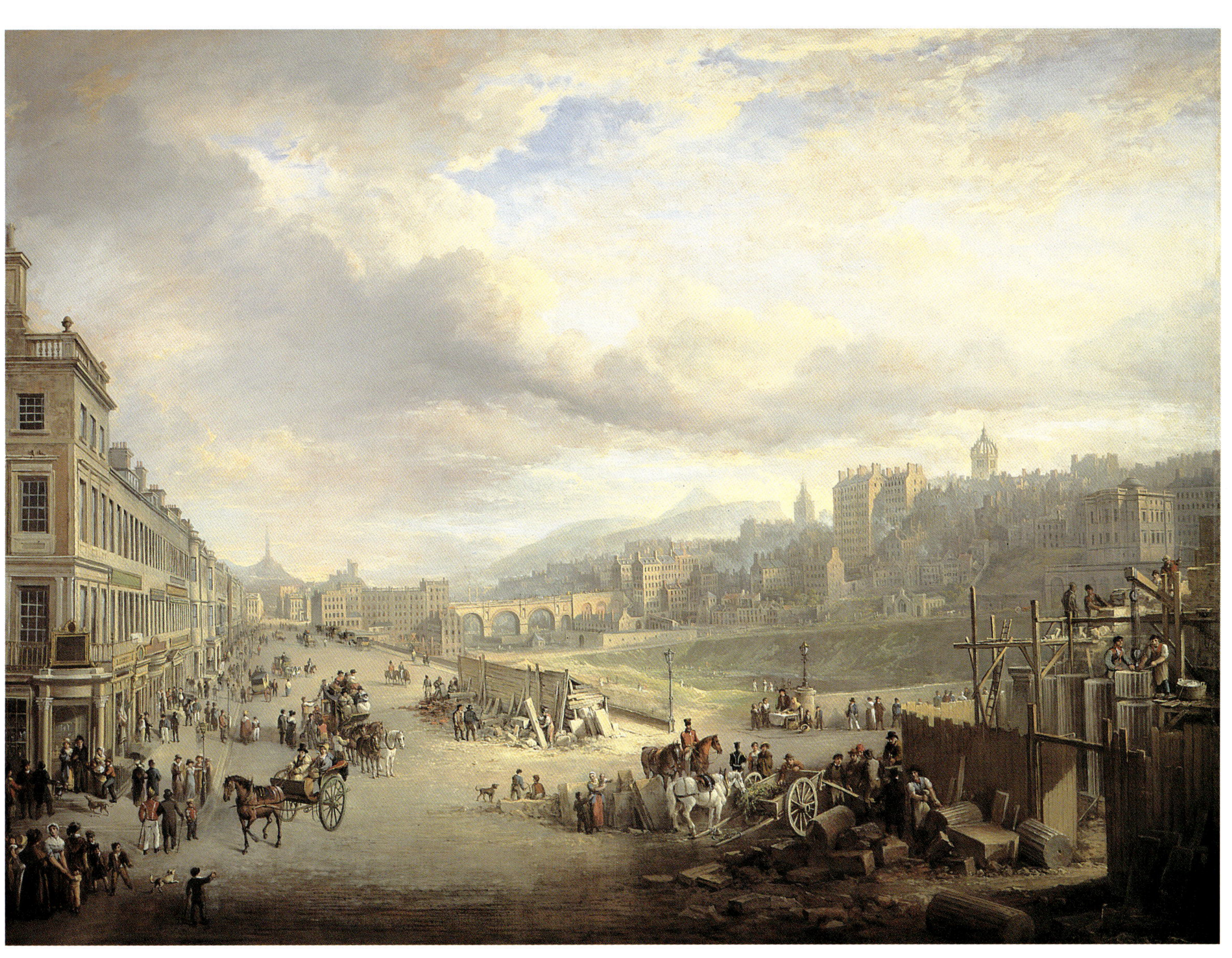

William Dyce 1806–1864
39 *King Lear and the Fool in the Storm*, exhibited 1851

Oil on canvas · 53½ × 68in (136 × 173cm)
Purchased with the aid of the National Art Collections Fund 1993
NG 2585

An Aberdonian by birth, Dyce was one of the most artistically gifted and intellectually able of the many Scottish painters who migrated to London in search of greater scope and international prestige. His wide range of interests, encompassing medicine, musicology, geology, ecclesiology and art education, has tended to obscure his stature as an easel painter and as the most competent British practitioner of fresco painting in the mid-nineteenth century. By vocation a religious and subject painter, he earned his living in the 1830s as a successful portrait painter in Edinburgh. In 1837, while teaching at the Trustees' Academy – established in the Scottish capital in 1760 as the earliest government-funded art school in Britain – he published his *Letter to Lord Meadowbank* on the reform of Scottish art education. The radicalism and intellectual vigour of this mission statement immediately earned Dyce an appointment as superintendent of the new School of Design at Somerset House in London.

The painting of *King Lear* (from *King Lear*, Act III, Scene 2), one of only two Shakespearian subjects to be treated by Dyce, coincided with the most intensive phase of the State-sponsored competitions for the mural decoration of the new Houses of Parliament. Official promotion of scenes from Shakespeare as the prime choice for illustration was based on an equation between Shakespearian drama and the ultimate cultural affirmation of British national identity. Between 1849 and 1852 a total of fifty-six Shakespearian pictures were shown at the Royal Academy, a phenomenon without precedent since Alderman John Boydell had launched his Shakespeare Gallery in 1786 as a commercial-cum-patriotic venture dedicated to the patronage of grand history painting (see M. Pointon, *William Dyce 1806–1864: A Critical Biography*, Oxford, 1979, pp.123, 165 and 199; J. Christian, *Shakespeare in Western Art*, British Council touring exhibition, Tokyo, 1992, cat.no.56).

During the 1850s Dyce was one of the few established artists to respond creatively to the aesthetic challenges presented by the young Pre-Raphaelites and to their hero-worship of Shakespeare. In 1851 Holman Hunt was invited to become Dyce's studio assistant. That same year Dyce's strikingly experimental *King Lear*, with its meticulous figure drawing and brilliant palette, was launched at the Royal Academy exhibition in proximity to Holman Hunt's illustration to *The Two Gentlemen of Verona* (Birmingham Museum and Art Gallery). Like Holman Hunt and Millais, Dyce sought to integrate figures painted in the studio into a localised landscape setting developed from sketches executed *en plein air*. Dyce's *King Lear* was purchased by John Knowles, the former proprietor of the Theatre Royal in Manchester following his prestigious appointment as manager of Her Majesty's Theatre in the Haymarket, London.

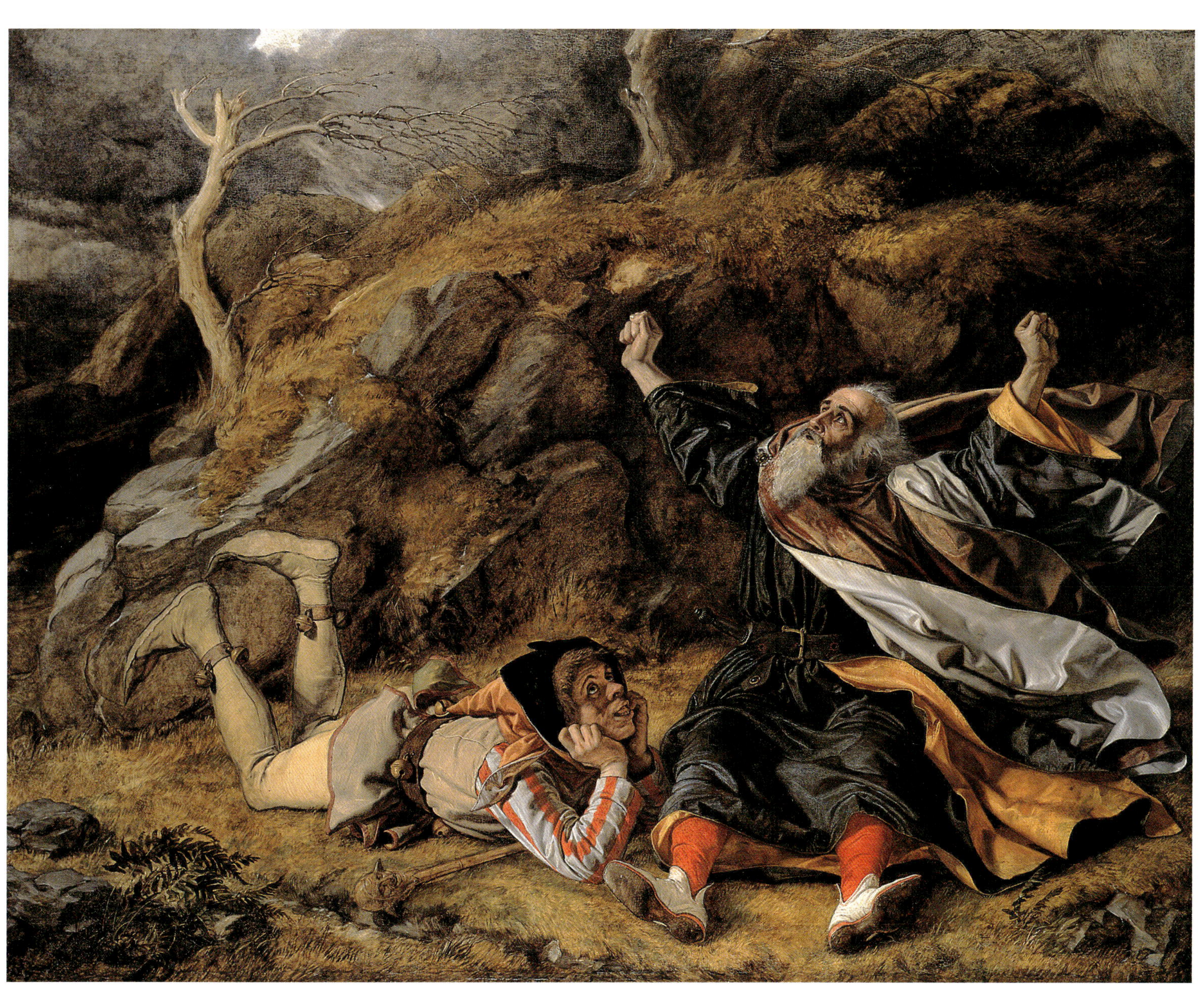

James Eckford Lauder 1811–1869

40 *James Watt and the Steam Engine: The Dawn of the Nineteenth Century*, 1855

Oil on canvas · 58 × 94in (147.3 × 238.7cm)
Signed twice in monogram bottom left
Purchased 1986
NG 2435

James Eckford Lauder and his older brother Robert Scott Lauder, later the most influential of all the masters of the Trustees' Academy, both belonged to the second generation of Scottish figure painters who benefited from the radical reform of this remarkable school of industrial and applied design founded in Edinburgh in 1760. In 1802 the elementary curriculum of the Trustees' drawing school had been extended through the introduction of oil painting, complemented by a system of annual premiums for the best historical composition in accordance with the practice of the Royal Academy Schools in London. During the 1820s Sir William Allan, the new Master of the Trustees' Academy, pioneered, under the influence of Sir Walter Scott, the painting of major pictures illustrative of Scottish history and literature. Among Allan's most gifted students were the Lauder brothers and James Drummond.

In general, contemporary industrial subjects were seldom favoured as themes for interpretative Scottish narrative painting. Eckford Lauder's choice of an eighteenth-century hero, the great Greenock-born inventor James Watt (1736–1819), as the subject of an epic history painting marked a unique departure from his usual specialisation in portraiture and in illustrations to Scott, Shakespeare and the Bible. This choice was prompted by the particularly momentous circumstances which obtained in 1855. That year the Royal Scottish Academy's suite of octagon galleries on the eastern side of Playfair's new dual-purpose National Gallery of Scotland building was completed just in time for the Academy's annual exhibition. Many of the exhibitors, including Eckford Lauder, made a special effort to mark this auspicious occasion.

By the 1850s Watt was perceived as an archetypal heroic figure of the inventor whose technical genius had harnessed the forces of nature and immeasurably advanced the progress of European civilisation. Eckford Lauder's picture complements perfectly the self-congratulatory and quasi-mythical literary commemoration of James Watt as a latter-day saint of the Industrial Revolution. The dramatic scale and composition of the painting deliberately invite comparison with Joseph Wright of Derby's illuminated night scenes depicting scientific experiments of which *An Experiment on a Bird in the Air Pump*, 1768 (National Gallery, London) is one of the best known and most spectacular (see ed. H. Fillitz, *Der Traum vom Glück. Die Kunst des Historismus in Europa*, exhibition catalogue, Künstlerhaus and Akademie der Bildenden Künste, Vienna, 1996, II, cat.no.18.13). Yet Lauder's specific subject has an appropriately Scottish context. Watt is depicted attempting to operate Glasgow University's defective Newcomen steam engine as an essential prelude to the innovations which were to bring him international renown.

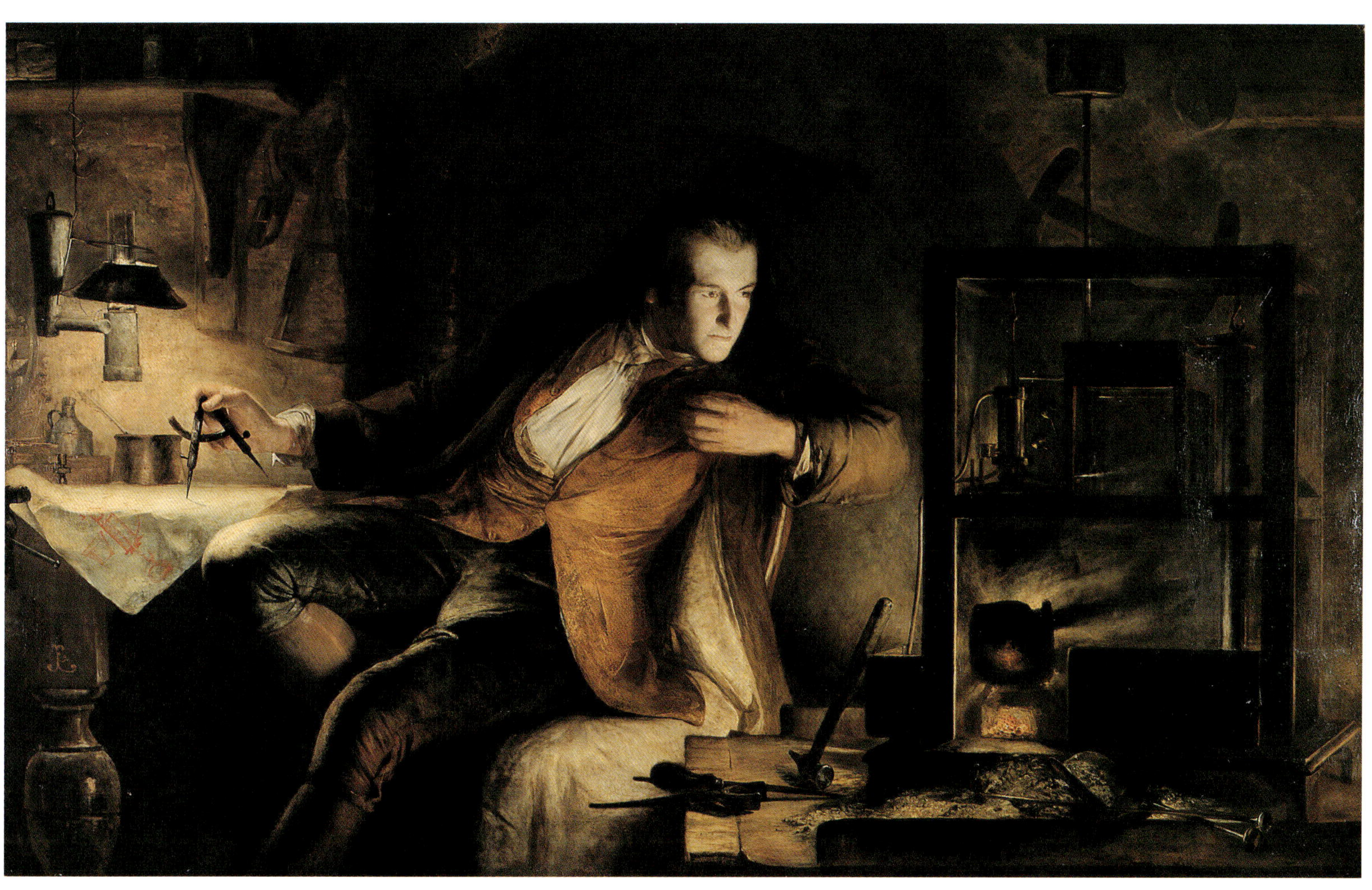

Horatio McCulloch 1805–1867

41 *Inverlochy Castle*, 1857

Oil on canvas · 35½ × 59½in (90.2 × 151cm)
Signed and dated bottom left: H. McCulloch 1857
Purchased by RAPFAS 1857; transferred to the National Gallery of Scotland 1897
NG 288

In 1829, after completing his formative studies with his fellow Glaswegian, the topographical and portrait painter John Knox, McCulloch began to exhibit at the Royal Scottish Academy in Edinburgh and in 1838 he settled permanently in the New Town there. By the late 1850s McCulloch occupied an extraordinary and almost messianic position in relation to Scottish landscape painting. McCulloch's capacity to distil the romantic essence of the Scottish landscape earned him both critical and popular acclaim as the northern counterpart of Constable and a truly representative 'national' painter, a status which depended on the unquestioning identification of Scotland with the Highlands. (See *The Discovery of Scotland: The Appreciation of Scottish Scenery Through Two Centuries of Painting*, exhibition catalogue, National Gallery of Scotland, Edinburgh, 1978, and *Horatio McCulloch 1805–1867*, exhibition catalogue, Glasgow Museums and Art Galleries, 1988).

McCulloch's grand Highland views were invariably composed in the studio from carefully prepared sketches executed on the spot in accordance with the common practice of all of his contemporaries. In 1856, during one of his regular summer sketching tours of the West Highlands, McCulloch made a watercolour study of Inverlochy Castle near Fort William. As originally displayed at the Royal Scottish Academy in 1857, the finished picture included in the foreground a group of Highland Cattle as picturesque localised detail. The substitution of an empty rowing boat as a device to strengthen the perspective of the composition may have been intended to intensify the general impression of isolation and desolation, relieved only by the presence of the crofters' cottages in the lee of the castle ruins.

From the 1840s McCulloch had benefited substantially from the steady support of the Edinburgh and Glasgow Art Unions. The Edinburgh association, founded in 1834 as the Royal Association for the Promotion of the Fine Arts in Scotland, was dedicated to the education of public taste and the patronage of contemporary Scottish painting through the outright purchase of original oils and the publication of related reproductive engravings. Each subscribing member of the Association was entitled to one set of the annual portfolio of engravings and a ticket for the prize lottery through which original works were distributed. In addition, a percentage of the subscription revenue was allocated to the formation of an independent collection of Scottish painting which was ultimately deposited in the National Gallery of Scotland. In 1857 RAPFAS purchased *Inverlochy Castle* from the Academy's exhibition for this definitive national collection. The engraving commissioned by RAPFAS in 1877 was designed as an illustration to *A Legend of Montrose* by Sir Walter Scott, thus emphasising the indebtedness of McCulloch's particular vision of the Highlands to the 'Wizard of the North'.

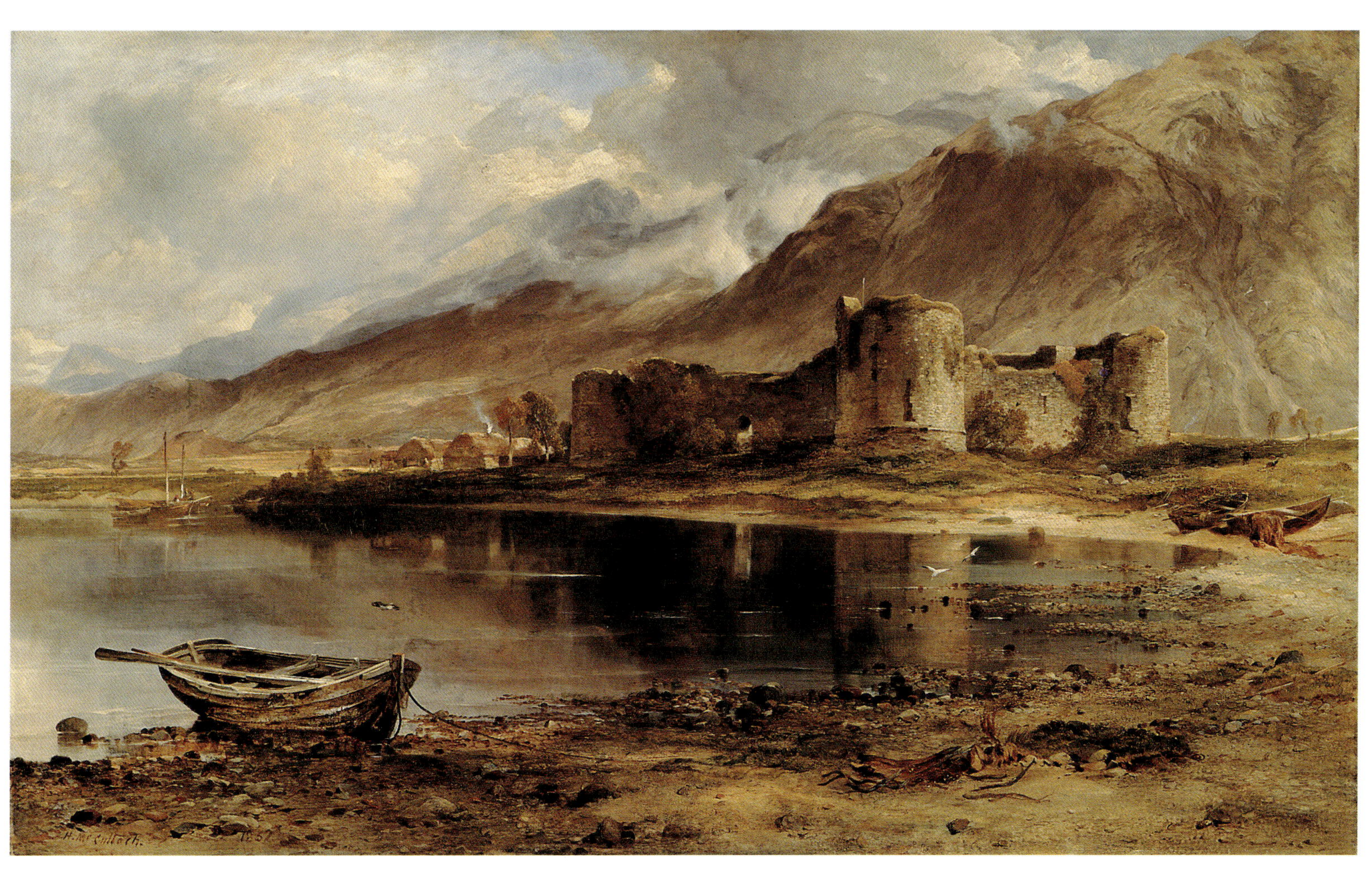
H. McCulloch.

James Drummond 1816–1877

42 ***Edinburgh, 16th June 1567 (later known as: The Return of Mary, Queen of Scots to Edinburgh)*, 1870**

Oil on canvas · 34 × 49¼in (86.4 × 125.1cm)
Signed and dated, lower left: J. Drummond. 1870
Bequest of the artist 1877
NG 625

Drummond's romantic and antiquarian approach towards the illustration of Scottish history was virtually predestined by his personal circumstances. Raised in the tenement in the High Street of Edinburgh known as John Knox's House, Drummond entered the Trustees' Academy as a student of Sir William Allan, the teacher of James Eckford Lauder. During the late 1840s, as a luminary of the Society of Antiquaries of Scotland, Drummond embarked on the meticulous documentation of the architecture and closes of the Old Town, many of the resulting drawings providing invaluable material for historical narrative painting. In 1856 the Royal Association for the Promotion of the Fine Arts in Scotland acknowledged both the centrality of history painting in the spectrum of contemporary Scottish art and Drummond's stature as one of its foremost practitioners by purchasing his most celebrated picture, *The Porteous Mob*, for the new National Gallery of Scotland. The artist himself set the seal upon this process by bequeathing the present picture to the Gallery of which he had become the second curator in 1868 in succession to his fellow history painter and antiquary, William Borthwick Johnstone.

The original title of the painting in the descriptive catalogue of the Royal Scottish Academy exhibition of 1870 referred quite specifically to the inauspicious day in June 1567 which marked the nadir of Mary Stewart's personal reign in Scotland. At the Battle of Carberry Hill on 15 June the royal troops had melted away before the massed ranks of the confederate Scottish lords, obliging their sovereign to surrender. While her ally the Earl of Bothwell retreated to Dunbar to await developments, Mary rode into Edinburgh in the vain anticipation of a parliamentary investigation of the rebels' grievances. Subjected to every indignity and to solitary confinement in the house of the Provost of Edinburgh, the queen was confronted by the lords' banner stationed before her window. It bore a crude accusatory image of her murdered husband Lord Darnley (see *James Drummond RSA. Victorian Antiquary and Artist of Old Edinburgh,* exhibition catalogue, City of Edinburgh Museums and Art Galleries, Edinburgh, 1977, cat.no.11 and H. Smailes and D. Thomson, *Mary Queen of Scots: The Queen's Image*, exhibition catalogue, National Galleries of Scotland, Edinburgh, 1987, cat.no.52).

Drummond focuses on the sequel to Carberry on 16 June 1567 and the ultimate humiliation of Mary, Queen of Scots. Ignoring the mocking invitation of the bystanders to trample upon the lords' banner, she contemplates the prospect of her imminent imprisonment in Lochleven Castle which was to culminate in her enforced abdication and, ultimately, in her execution. The actual and implicit drama is played out against an elaborate period stage set. Demolished in 1788, the Black Turnpike was one of the most sumptuous buildings in the High Street of Edinburgh and was traditionally associated with Sir Simon Preston, the Provost in 1567. In 1870 Drummond reconstructed this building in his picture, adding the carved initials and coat of arms in order to complete the illusion.

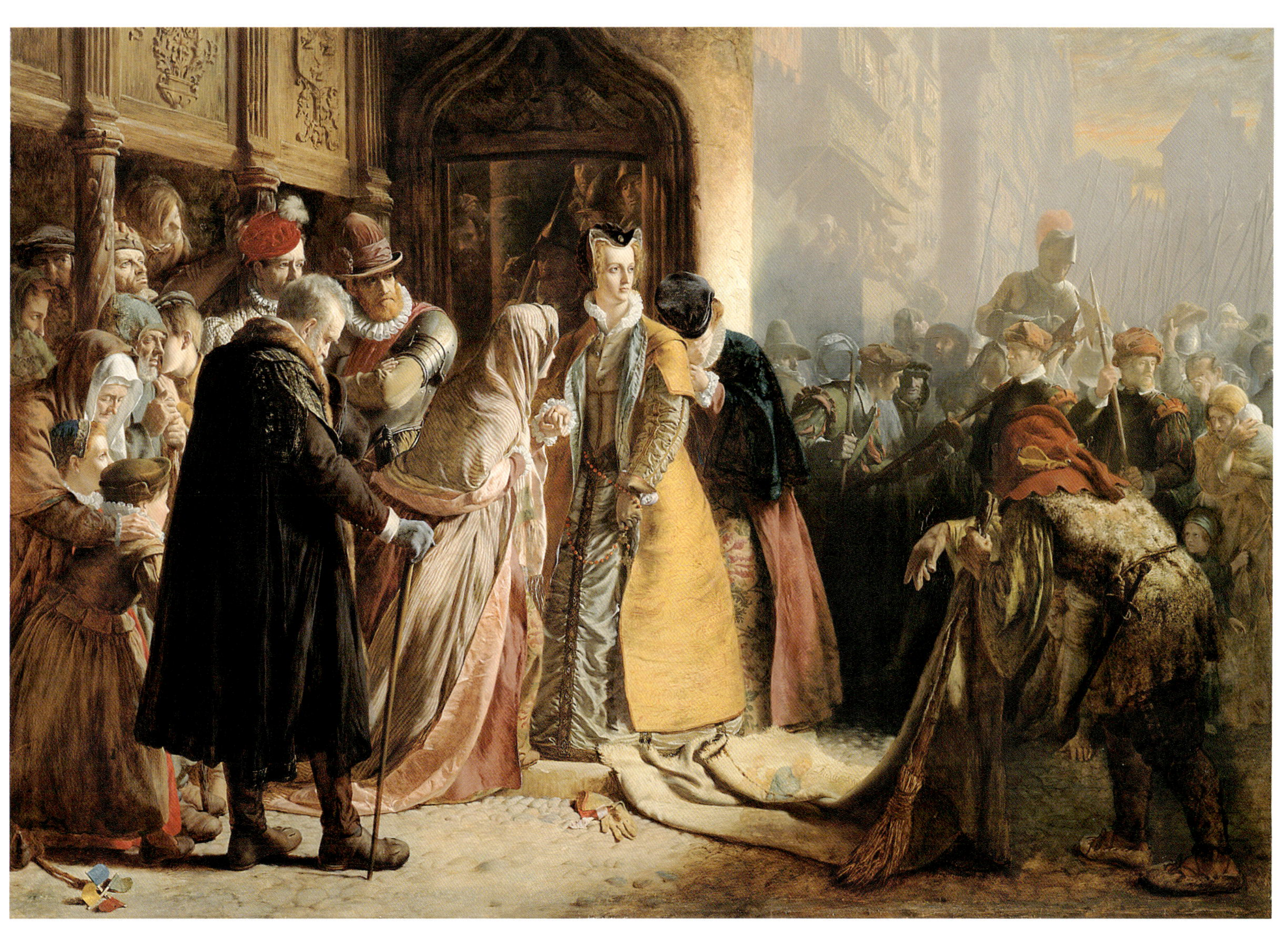

William McTaggart 1835–1910

43 *Machrihanish Bay*, 1878

Oil on canvas · 32½ × 48½in (82.5 × 123.2cm)
Signed and dated, lower right: W. McTaggart/1878
Presented by Mr and Mrs D.W.T. Cargill 1938
NG 1906

McTaggart's lifelong technical and conceptual progress towards achieving a complete unification of all the diverse elements in pictorial composition can be traced from stage to stage through the most representative public collection of his work, which is held by the National Gallery of Scotland. A brilliant student of Robert Scott Lauder at the Trustees' Academy in Edinburgh during the 1850s, McTaggart was to remain first and foremost a figure painter in his own estimation. Throughout his career he experimented incessantly with different ways of combining figures and an independently executed landscape setting. As late as 1890, when he completed *The Storm*, the narrative element was still predominant, his subject on this occasion being essentially the fragility and resilience of human resistance pitted against massive and violent natural forces. Purchased by Andrew Carnegie as a tour de force of McTaggart's landscape painting in 1901, *The Storm* was presented to the Gallery in 1935 by Carnegie's widow in commemoration of the dual centenary of the birth of the artist and of his patron and as a permanent tribute to Scotland's most potent and expressive painter of the sea.

McTaggart's principal biographer and champion, Sir James Lewis Caw, ranked his father-in-law as the equal of J.M.W. Turner as a marine artist, endowed 'with a passion and insight, a profound knowledge of Nature and an assured mastery of expression, which makes him incomparable. Other men paint the form and colour of the sea; he expresses its apparent life' (see J.L. Caw, *William McTaggart* RSA, VPRSW. *A Biography and an Appreciation*, Glasgow, 1917, vol.II, pp.164–5). From 1883 the vigour and immediacy of McTaggart's response to the sea and to the fleeting effects of wind and weather – a fascination which the Scottish artist shared with Constable whose landscapes he studied at every opportunity – were to be intensified by his practice of painting the majority of his canvases out of doors and directly from nature in Kintyre and the Isle of Arran in the west and, on the east coast of Scotland, at Carnoustie. Situated on the bleak west coast of Kintyre and exposed to the full force of the Atlantic, Machrihanish Bay offers the longest continuous stretch of sand in Argyll. The fluid handling of this pure landscape, a transitional work painted in 1878, its long horizontal rhythms and deftly placed accents (such as the brown seaweed on the shore and the white flicks of the breaking wave) suggest the influence of Whistler and, in particular, of his famous *Nocturnes* (see *William McTaggart 1835–1910*, exhibition catalogue, National Galleries of Scotland, Edinburgh, 1989, p.61 and cat.no.45). In 1877 and 1878 several Whistlers were exhibited at the Grosvenor Gallery in London, then the principal venue for the display and promotion of avant-garde British art, where McTaggart may first have encountered the painting of his radical American contemporary.

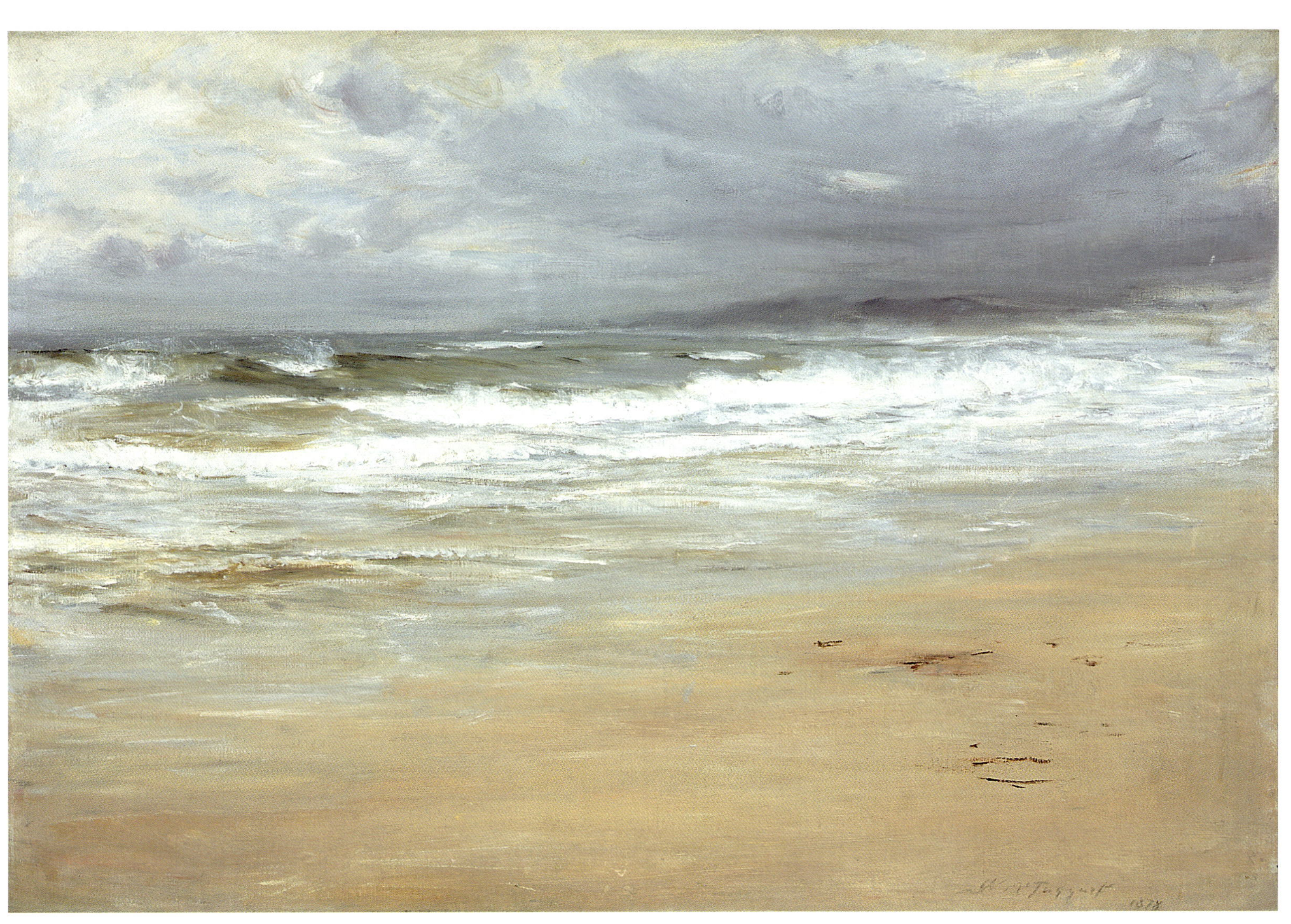

Sir Joshua Reynolds 1723–1792

44 *Alexander Douglas-Hamilton, later 10th Duke of Hamilton and 7th Duke of Brandon*, 1782

Oil on canvas · 27 × 21½in (68.5 × 55cm)
Presented by Elspeth Tullis, Lady Invernairn of Strathnairn; received after her death 1956
NG 2183

Over the summer of 1781 Reynolds left London for the Low Countries on one of his rare excursions abroad since his critical visit to Italy in 1749–1752. His prolonged exposure to Italian painting of the High Renaissance and the seventeenth century had deeply and lastingly affected his own practice in portraiture and history painting and his general ideology of art which was subsequently expounded in his *Discourses* to the Royal Academy during the 1760s. His renewed encounter with the portraiture of Rubens in 1781 was immediately reflected in this engaging portrait of the fourteen-year-old Alexander Douglas-Hamilton (1767–1852), painted the following year at the beginning of the final productive decade of the artist's career.

Reynolds owed this portrait commission to the connoisseur-collector William Beckford of Fonthill who was to marry Hamilton's cousin in 1783 and whose own daughter and co-heiress by that marriage, Susan Euphemia, would become Hamilton's wife in 1810 (see *Sir Joshua Reynolds 1723–1792*, exhibition catalogue, Royal Academy, London, 1986, cat.no.131 and D. Mannings, *Sir Joshua Reynolds. A Complete Catalogue of His Paintings*, New Haven and London, 2000, cat.no.807). Both a practising homosexual and a zealous genealogist, Beckford may well have been equally attracted to Hamilton by the physical charm of his distant relative and future son-in-law and by the hauteur of his demeanour which an obituarist would ascribe in 1852 to 'a great predisposition to over-estimate the importance of ancient birth'. In his maturity, as 10th Duke of Hamilton and premier peer of Scotland, Hamilton claimed to be the legitimate heir to the Scottish throne, the direct Stewart line of succession having ended in 1807.

Apart from his overbearing dynastic pride, Hamilton's most distinguishing feature was the passion for collecting which he shared with Beckford, a substantial part of whose French collection he either purchased or inherited. In his own collecting Hamilton sought to emulate, on an appropriately regal scale, the example of George IV who, when Prince Regent, had formed the most extensive collection of French art in Britain. At Hamilton Palace in Lanarkshire the Duke assembled the most outstanding French collection ever to be conceived in Scotland including furniture and *objets d'art* associated with the French royal family, the Emperor Napoleon and his sister Princess Pauline Borghese (see the essay by G. Evans, 'The Great Collectors' in *French Connections: Scotland & the Arts of France*, exhibition catalogue, Royal Scottish Museum, Edinburgh, 1985, pp.71–102). By the time he inherited the Dukedom in 1819, Alexander Douglas-Hamilton had been a serious collector for twenty years. He was therefore pre-eminently qualified to serve as a Commissioner of the Board of Trustees for Manufactures in Scotland which, from 1850, would be entrusted with the management of the newly-constituted National Gallery of Scotland and which, since 1760, had administered the art school in Edinburgh known as the Trustees' Academy. During the most intensive phase of his private collecting, Hamilton also served as Vice-President of the Institution for the Encouragement of the Fine Arts in Scotland whose collection of Old Master painting was ultimately vested in the Gallery.

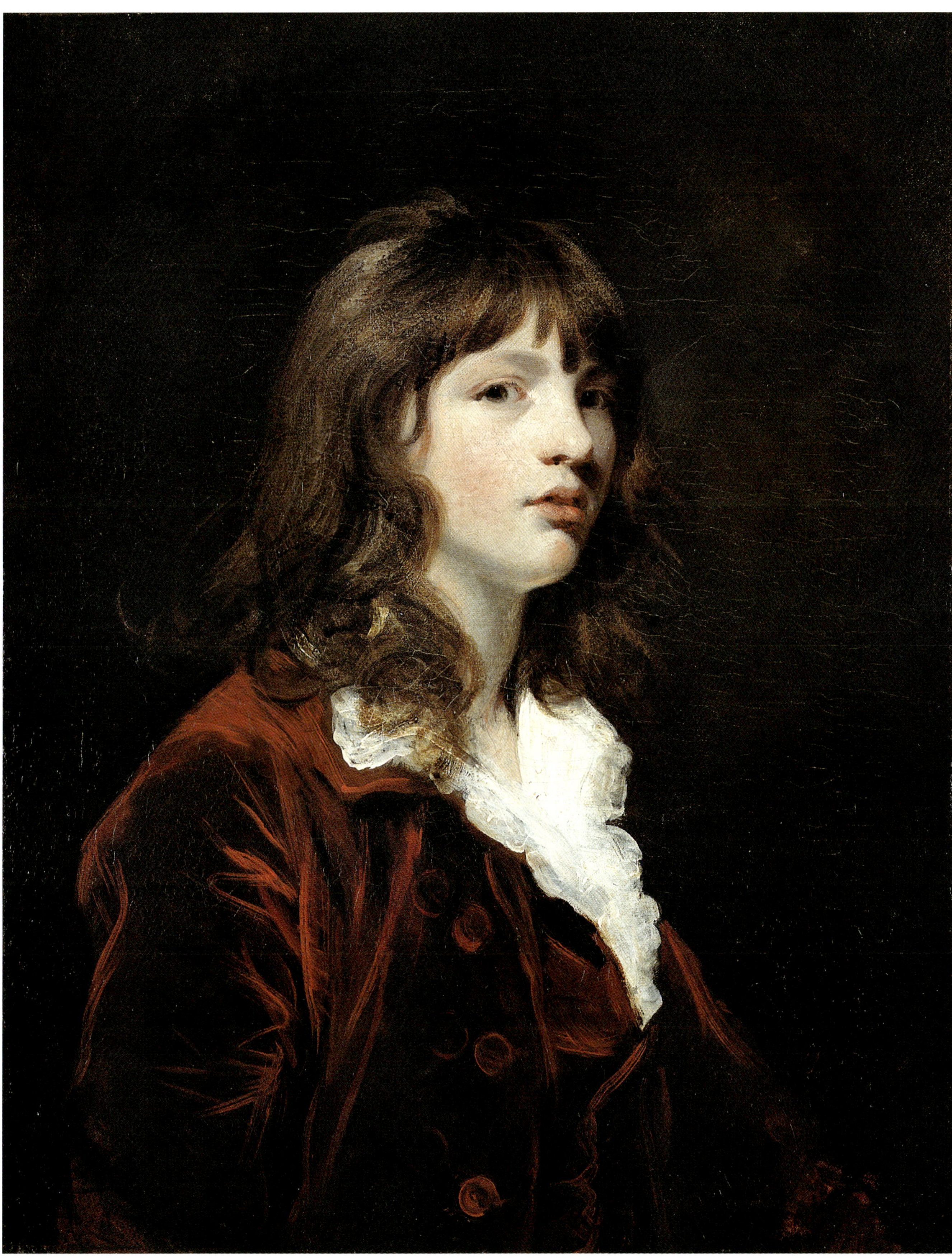

Thomas Gainsborough 1727–1788

45 *Rocky Landscape*, exhibited 1783

Oil on canvas · 47 × 58in (119.4 × 147.3cm)
Purchased with the aid of a Treasury Grant 1962
NG 2253

By the mid-1770s the fashionable spa town of Bath, where Gainsborough had settled in 1759, had ceased to provide an adequate clientele for his portraiture. In 1774 he made a strategic move to Schomberg House in central London in the immediate vicinity of the earliest premises to be occupied by the Royal Academy on the south side of Pall Mall. The chief promoter and most eloquent exponent of the artistic policy of the Academy, founded in 1768 under the patronage of George III, was Gainsborough's arch-rival in portraiture, Sir Joshua Reynolds. Having quarrelled with the Academy in 1773, Gainsborough did not exhibit there again until 1777 and his political relationship with the institution was to remain ambivalent despite his status as a founder-member. Yet it was from Reynolds, as President of the Academy, that he would receive one of the most sensitive posthumous tributes to his own achievements as a landscape painter.

About 1764 Gainsborough wrote to his patron Lord Hardwicke that, 'with respect to *real Views* from Nature in this Country he [Gainsborough] has never seen any Place that affords a Subject equal to the poorest imitations of Gaspar or Claude.' By identifying himself firmly with the Old Master tradition of ideal landscape painting, Gainsborough declared simultaneously his complete lack of interest in purely descriptive topography. Almost twenty years later, he undertook the by then fashionable tour of the Lake District, his aim being 'to mount all the Lakes at the next Exhibition, in the great stile'. *Rocky Landscape*, probably exhibited at the Royal Academy in 1783 and thus painted immediately before this tour, was the first of a series of 'sublime' mountain landscapes in which he strove to attain a wild grandeur reminiscent of the seventeenth-century Roman painters Salvator Rosa and Gaspard Dughet (see J. Hayes, *The Landscape Paintings of Thomas Gainsborough*, London, 1982, II, pp.501–3, cat.no.137). Gainsborough's complex integration of immediate observation from nature with allusive re-interpretation of the conventions of the Italian and French Old Master tradition earned the ultimate accolade from Reynolds. In his fourteenth public *Discourse* to the students of the Royal Academy, Reynolds confessed to being captivated both by 'the powerful impression of nature, which Gainsborough exhibited in his portraits and in his landskips' and by the 'genius' of this rival who had excelled in 'the lower rank of art'.

In spite of its exceptional quality, *Rocky Landscape* remained unsold in Gainsborough's studio until 1789 when it was purchased at the artist's posthumous sale by Earl Gower, Marquess of Stafford. Lord Gower, later created 1st Duke of Sutherland, inherited both the Stafford and the Bridgewater pictures which, collectively, formed the most outstanding private collection of Old Master painting in Britain outside the Royal Collection. The Gainsborough remained in family possession until its acquisition by the Gallery in 1953 when it was reunited, quite fortuitously, with the finest of the Stafford and Bridgewater pictures lent to the Gallery in 1945 by the Duke of Sutherland.

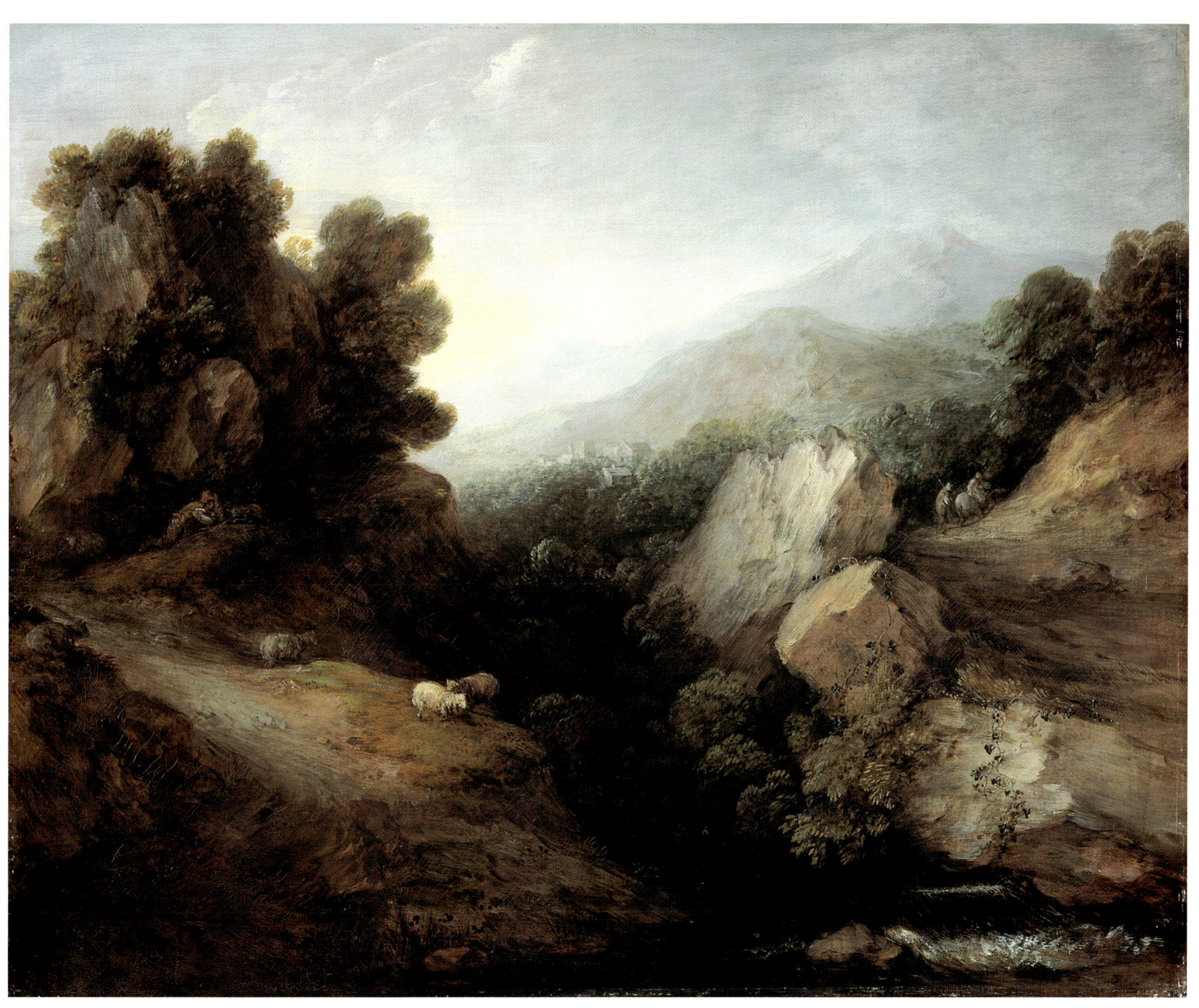

John Crome 1768–1821

46 *The Beaters*, *c*.1810

Oil on panel · 21½ × 34in (54.6 × 86.4cm)
Purchased 1970
NG 2309

In 1803 a Society of Artists was established in Norwich in the county of Norfolk and East Anglia 'for the purpose of investigating the rise, progress, decline and revival of the fine arts', the first regional exhibiting association of its kind in England. Until the late eighteenth century Norwich was one of the most prosperous English provincial towns, second only to Bristol and York, its prosperity having been founded upon the woollen industry and related trading connections with the Low Countries which had been operational since the Middle Ages. From 1805 the Society's annual exhibitions provided the focus for a distinctive 'School' of painting. Dominant representatives of this Norwich School were John Sell Cotman (1782–1842), who set up a School for Drawing and Design in the town in 1806, and John Crome senior, a local drawing-master and former sign-painter, who, together with his brother-in-law Robert Ladbrooke, had founded the Society of Artists.

Although Crome's subject matter was invariably the local landscape and was consequently invested with a compelling immediacy of appeal, his work was frequently criticised for its 'unfinished' appearance even towards the end of his career. Yet, within weeks of Crome's death, a correspondent of the sculptor John Flaxman informed him that East Anglian collectors were 'crazy for his pictures'. Among the later devotees of the Norwich artist was J.N. Sherrington of Great Yarmouth who purchased exclusively paintings by Crome, on occasion from some of his original patrons, and from whose collection *The Beaters* was sold in 1858. At the time of this sale the previous owner was identified as John Bracey, another Yarmouth collector, one of whose specially commissioned Crome landscapes – conceivably *The Beaters* – had been advertised for sale by Bracey's executors in the *Norwich Mercury* in 1835 with the collaboration of the artist's son John Berney Crome and extolled as 'a *chef d'oeuvre* of the Master' (see D. and T. Clifford, *John Crome*, London, 1968, pp.67, 207–208, 249, 274–275 and cat.no.P56; N. Goldberg, *John Crome the Elder*, Oxford, 1978, vol.I, pp.24 and 191–192, cat.no.43).

The elder Crome is not known to have signed his pictures and the precise chronological sequence of his work is difficult to determine. In 1969 a putative 'signature' and the date 1810 were removed during conservation of *The Beaters*, although the approximate dating is still considered to be appropriate. (The questionable inscription has been associated with the dating first proposed by C.H. Collins Baker in his monograph *Crome*, Dundee, 1921. See also the sources listed above.) The compositional motif of a woodland scene with gnarled tree trunks, tufted foliage and small figures, and the textural treatment of the muddy path are strongly reminiscent of seventeenth-century Dutch landscapes by Hobbema and Ruisdael whose work Crome had studied at first hand in his youth in the collection of his friend Thomas Harvey.

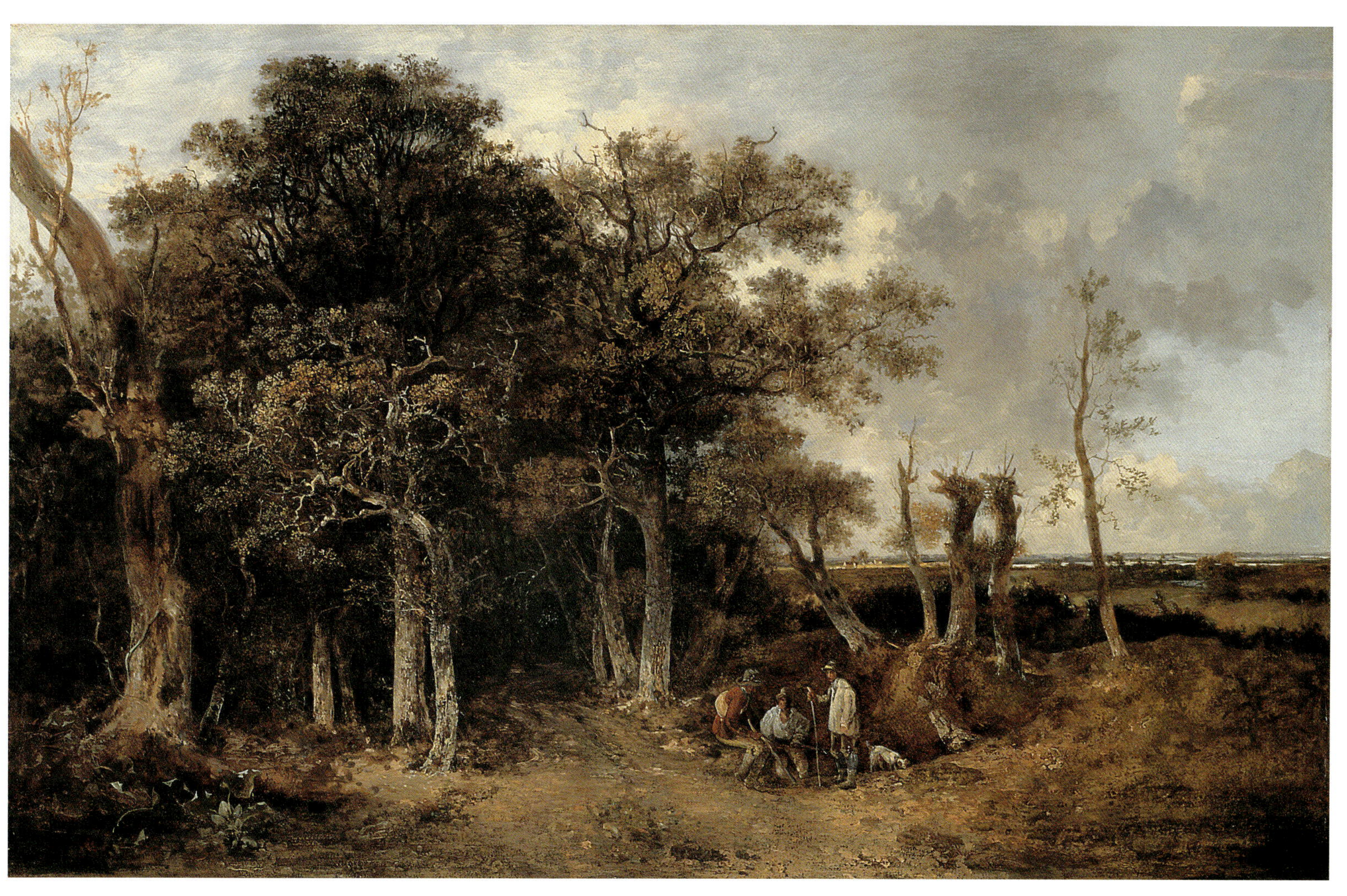

Sir Thomas Lawrence 1769–1830

47 *Mary Digges, Lady Robert Manners*, exhibited 1826

Oil on canvas · 54½ × 43½in (138.5 × 110.5cm)
Bequest of Mrs Nisbet Hamilton Ogilvy 1921
NG 1522

In his Edinburgh lectures delivered in 1853 the critic John Ruskin recounted a fascinating anecdote of the first appearance of the painting of Lady Manners (1737–1829) in London at the Royal Academy exhibition of 1826. As a conciliatory gesture towards the mortified Lawrence, J. M.W. Turner allegedly applied a temporary wash of lamp black to his own high-keyed picture of Cologne whose proximity to Lawrence's portrait had had 'a most injurious effect'. Such deference towards Lawrence, even on the part of Turner, reflected Sir Thomas's cultural-political pre-eminence as President of the Royal Academy and his unchallenged position as the leading portrait painter in Europe.

Lawrence owed both of these distinctions in equal measure to his own exceptional flair and ability, and to the sustained and committed patronage of the Prince Regent who succeeded to the throne as George IV in 1820, the year of Sir Thomas's election to the presidency. The knighthood conferred upon him in 1815 provided the social status commensurate with the Prince Regent's commission for a series of portraits of the European monarchs, statesmen and generals then in alliance with Britain against Napoleon. Lawrence's royal mission to the Continent, whose progress was delayed by the escape of Napoleon from Elba, culminated in Rome in 1819 with the execution of full-length portraits of Pius VII and his chief minister Cardinal Consalvi.

As a masterly production of Lawrence's maturity and one endowed with an unusually powerful characterisation of a female sitter, *Lady Manners* attracted remarkably little critical attention in 1826 beyond the predictable 'sentiments of respect' elicited by the advanced age and formidable personality of the sitter (*Sir Thomas Lawrence 1769–1830*, exhibition catalogue, National Portrait Gallery, London, 1979, cat.no.46 and K. Garlick, *Sir Thomas Lawrence: A Complete Catalogue of his Paintings*, Oxford, 1989, cat.no.541). Lady Manners's portrait continued to grace the family collection until 1921 when the National Galleries of Scotland received a major bequest from her lineal descendant, Mrs Nisbet Hamilton Ogilvy of Biel in East Lothian. Among the corpus of family portraits were the Ramsay and the Lawrence of Mary Digges and a captivating half-length of her granddaughter Mary Nisbet, Countess of Elgin, painted by Baron Gérard in Paris. This bequest added a total of thirty-two portraits and Old Master paintings to the national collections, including *The Tribute Money* by Serodine, the *Fantastic Landscape* by Paul Bril, and two Venetian views by Guardi, while simultaneously fulfilling the benefactor's secondary intention of depriving her heir of entail of any substantial pictorial legacy.

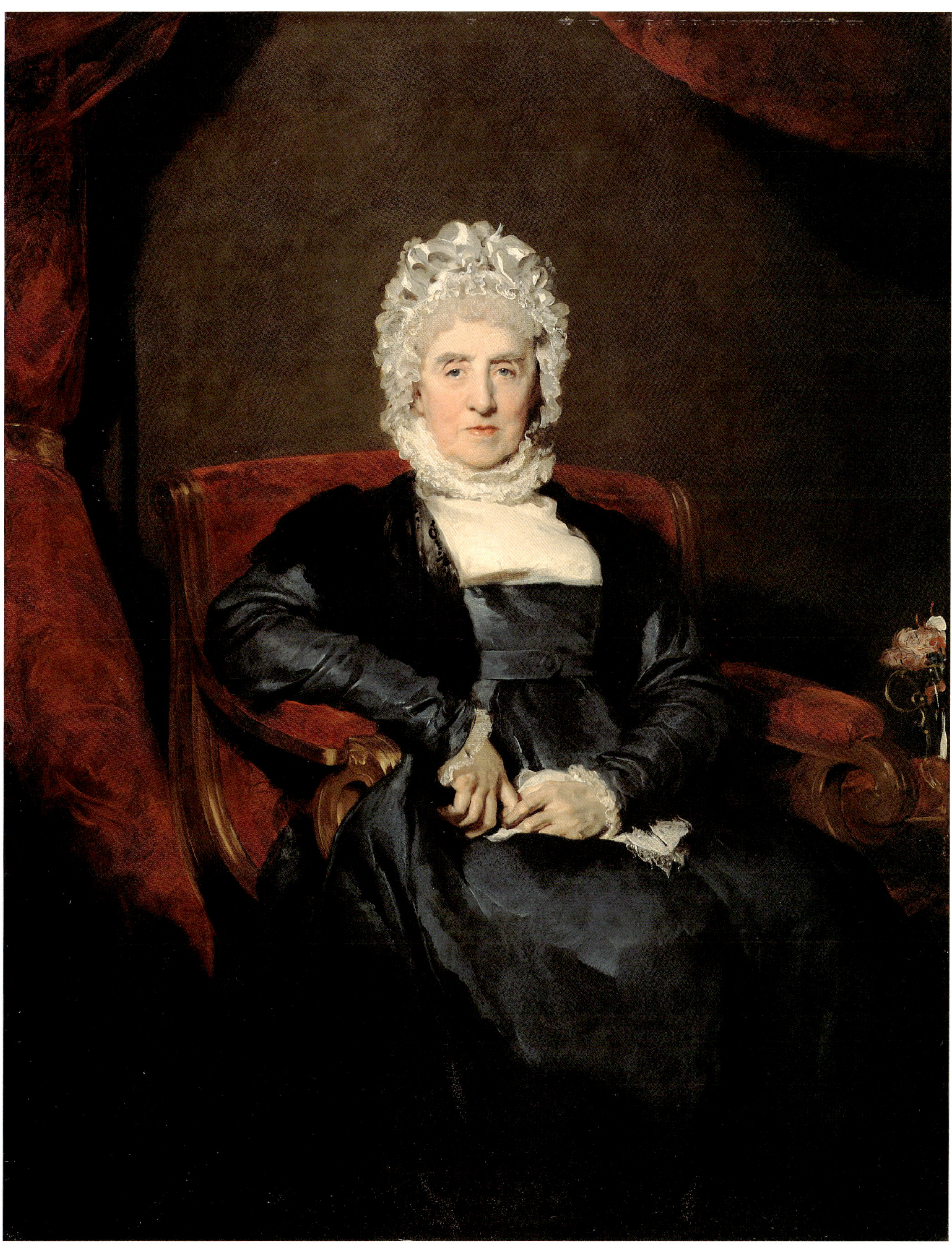

John Constable 1776–1837

48 *The Vale of Dedham*, 1828

Oil on canvas · 56⅞ × 48in (144.5 × 122cm)
Purchased with the Cowan Smith Bequest Fund
with additional assistance from the National Art Collections Fund 1944
NG 2016

Among his British contemporaries, including his great rival J. M.W. Turner, Constable was exceptional in never venturing overseas and remaining passionately committed to the intensive observation and celebration of the fertile countryside within a few miles' radius of his native village of East Bergholt in Suffolk. In 1827, after almost a decade of flitting between city and country, he acquired a permanent lease on a house in Well Walk, Hampstead, on the northern outskirts of the city of London which commanded a spectacular urban prospect 'unequalled in Europe'. Later that year he took his two eldest children on their first visit to East Bergholt, a pilgrimage which provided an emotive opportunity for reflection on his profound artistic engagement with the local landscape. For the Royal Academy exhibition of 1828 and his 'best' picture, his passport to election as an Academician in 1829, Constable resolved on the definitive treatment of a subject which had preoccupied him for over twenty years – the view from Gun Hill (now called Langham Coombe), looking down the Stour Valley towards the distinctive perpendicular tower of the church at Dedham, where his father worked a watermill, and beyond towards the port of Harwich and the Stour estuary. This was to be his last major view of the Stour Valley (see *Constable, Paintings, Watercolours & Drawings*, exhibition catalogue, Tate Gallery, London, 1976, pp.151–2, cat.no.253 and G. Reynolds, *The Later Paintings and Drawings of John Constable*, New Haven and London 1984, pp.189–90, cat.no.28.1).

In the letterpress to his important print series *English Landscape*, published between 1830 and 1832, Constable confessed that, 'every recollection associated with the Vale of Dedham must always be dear to [me] … It was [there] that the Author's ideas of Landscape were formed; and he dwells on the retrospect of those happy days … with a fondness and delight which must ever be to him a source of happiness and contentment.' In 1802, when he had first dedicated himself to 'natural painture', he had painted a smaller upright landscape (Victoria and Albert Museum, London) from a viewpoint identical to that in *Dedham Vale.* The later picture, with its subtle representation of fleeting showers and flashing sunlight, marks the climax of his lifelong quest 'to render permanent … those splendid but evanescent exhibitions … of external Nature' (see *Constable's Clouds*, exhibition catalogue, National Galleries of Scotland and National Museums and Galleries on Merseyside, 2000, cat.no.173). Yet Constable's credo of 'pure and unaffected representation' did not exclude selective assimilation of the Old Master tradition of landscape painting in which Gainsborough, for whom Constable felt a particular admiration and affinity, was also steeped. The composition of both the 1802 and the 1828 Dedham landscapes was partially modelled upon *Hagar and the Angel* by Claude Lorrain, the most treasured possession of Sir George Beaumont and one of the Beaumont pictures subsequently acquired by the National Gallery in London. Sir George having died in 1827, Constable may well have decided to revive his own Claudian composition the following year as a tribute to his longstanding friend and patron.

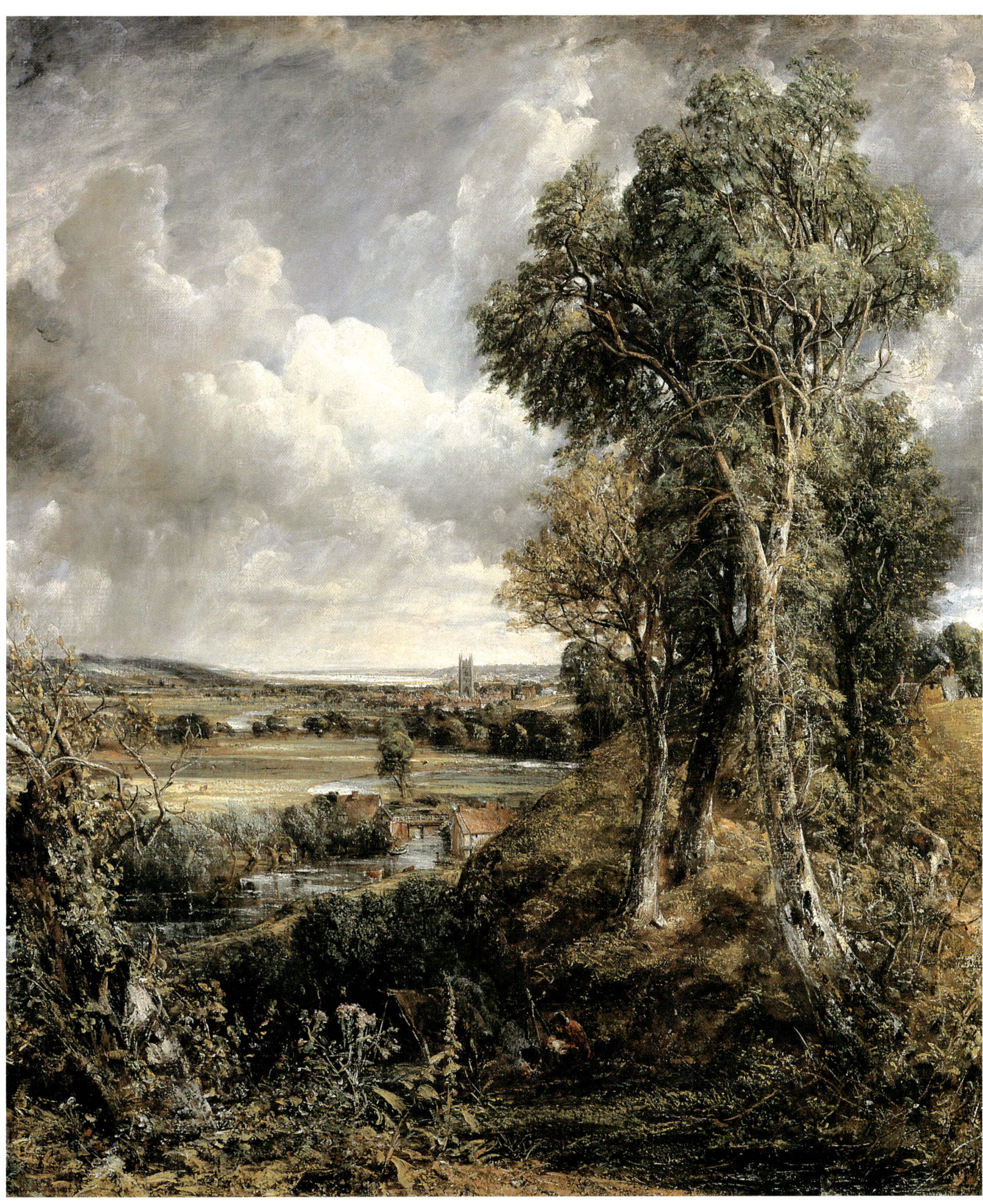

Sir Edwin Henry Landseer 1802–1873

49 *Rent-Day in the Wilderness*, 1868

Oil on canvas · 48 × 104½in (122 × 265cm)
Bequest of Sir Roderick Impey Murchison 1871
NG 586

By 1855, when he initially approached Landseer with this most unusual commission for a Scottish history painting, Sir Roderick Impey Murchison, President of the Royal Geographical Society and the supremely distinguished British geologist of his day, had already enlisted the assistance of two other artists in producing his own rendering of the heroic exploits of his great-grandfather Colonel Donald Murchison in the service of the Mackenzies of Kintail, originally the senior branch of the Clan Mackenzie. Landseer, then at the height of his reputation and the recent recipient of a knighthood from Queen Victoria, had first visited Scotland in 1824 with the history painter and writer C.R. Leslie. Following a momentous encounter with Sir Walter Scott, Landseer was commissioned to contribute illustrations to Cadell's edition of the Waverley Novels. The artist's impassioned enthusiasm for Scotland, which he indulged during annual shooting, hunting and sketching trips from 1825, is now popularly identified with his single most spectacular Highland sporting picture *The Monarch of the Glen*, in the collection of United Distillers.

Sir Roderick himself, a native of Easter Ross and of Mackenzie descent on his mother's side, chose to model for the figure of Colonel Murchison. In 1715, following the defeat of the Jacobite army of the Old Pretender, James Francis Edward Stewart, at Sherriffmuir, his supporter the Earl of Seaforth was subject to attainder for high treason, whereby he forfeited his civil rights, his title and the legal ownership of his estates. While the Earl sought refuge in France, the management of the confiscated Mackenzie estates in Ross-shire was entrusted to Colonel Murchison. The Colonel, in the guise of his great-grandson, is depicted at Aa na Mullich in 1722, collecting rents from the Mackenzie tenants in defiance of the law for eventual despatch to his exiled master in Paris, while other tenants observe through telescopes the movements of a hostile party of Hanoverian redcoats beyond Loch Affric. As late as 1725 the English General Wade complained to George I that Murchison had travelled to Edinburgh unmolested in order to arrange an illegal remittance to Seaforth. Despite his dedicated loyalty, Murchison is alleged to have been ungratefully treated when the attainted earl was repossessed of his estates, and to have died of a broken heart (see *Sir Edwin Landseer*, exhibition catalogue, Philadelphia Museum of Art and Tate Gallery, London, 1982, cat.no.155).

Completion of the picture was delayed for over a decade on account of other outstanding or more prestigious commitments including a government commission to Landseer for four bronze lions to flank Nelson's Column in Trafalgar Square. Landseer's Scottish history painting was finally delivered to his sorely tried patron in time for the Royal Academy exhibition of 1868.

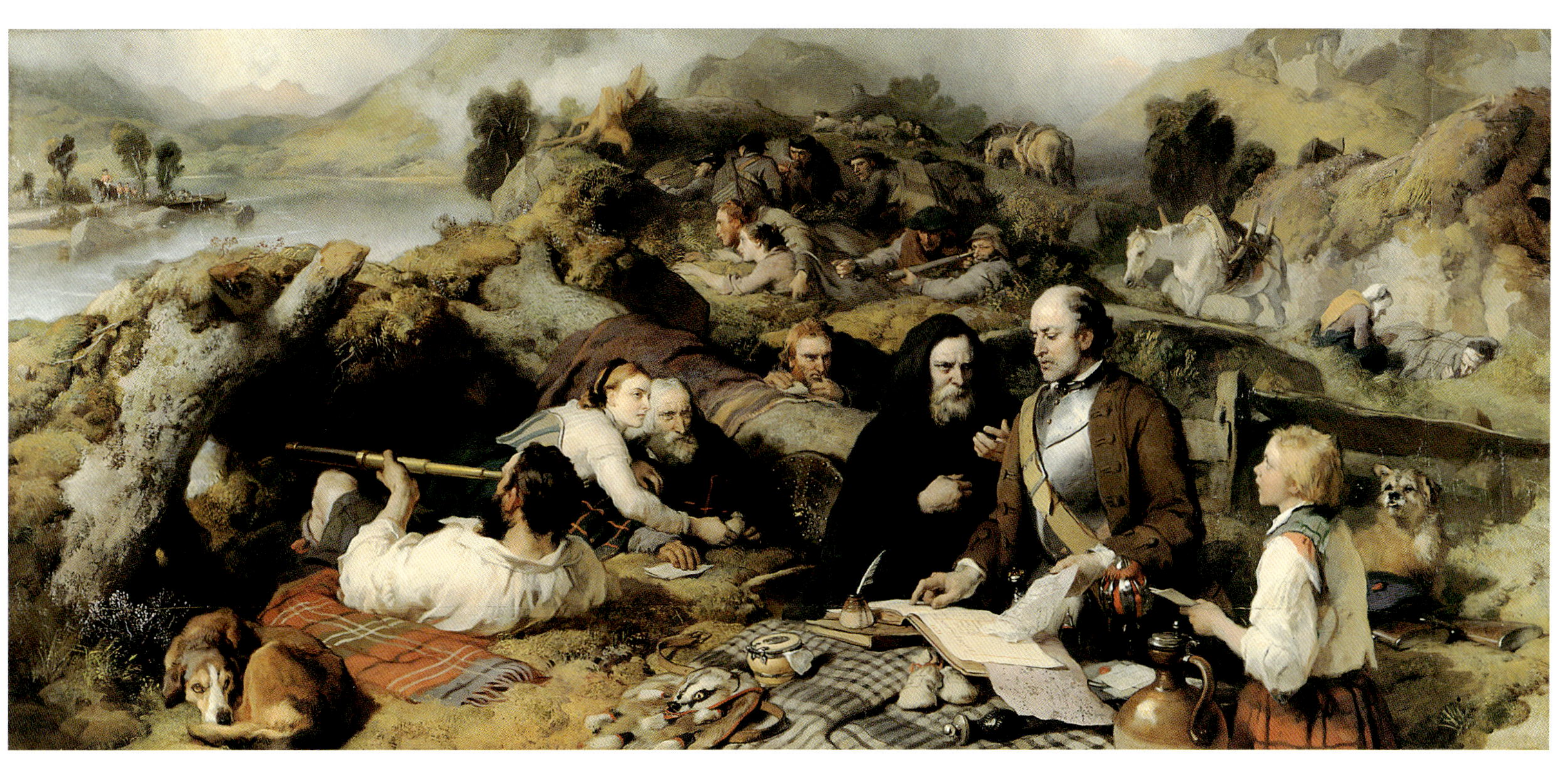

Frederic Edwin Church 1826–1900

50 *Niagara Falls from the American Side*, 1867

Oil on canvas · 102½ x 91in (260 x 231cm)
Signed and dated, lower right: F. E. Church / 1867
Presented by John S.Kennedy 1887
NG 799

In 1844, through the intermediary of Daniel Wadsworth, the Connecticut collector and founder of the Wadsworth Athenaeum in his native Hartford, Church became the first and, ultimately, the most distinguished student to be accepted by Thomas Cole (1801–1848). In his *Essay on American Scenery* of 1835 the founder of the Hudson River School, the first truly indigenous American school of painting, had exhorted his fellow Americans to discover the sublime beauty of their own country and to marvel at the divine handiwork in natural wonders such as Niagara, one of the defining landmarks of North America. The landscape tradition which Cole developed was to be perpetuated well into the twentieth century. Church began exhibiting independently at the National Academy of Design and the American Art Union while still attending Cole's studio at Catskill and in 1847 he settled permanently in New York.

This view of Niagara Falls, a symbolic national landmark, looks across the American Falls, past Goat Island, to the Horseshoe or Canadian Falls with the Canadian shore on the far side. The observation platform in the lower left was apparently invented by Church, and the figures he depicted in it were probably his friend Erasmus Dow Palmer (1817–1903) and his daughter Madeleine. Dwarfed as they are by the mighty falls, their diminutive presence serves only to emphasise the mighty forces of nature unleashed before them.

It is highly unusual to find such a spectacular American nineteenth-century landscape painting in a European public collection. The circumstances of its arrival in Scotland are as follows. It was acquired in 1887 by John Stewart Kennedy (1830–1909) who had emigrated to the United States from his native Scotland at the age of seventeen. He amassed a considerable fortune in iron and coal and was an important figure in the New York business and social world, as well as being an art lover and philanthropist. Kennedy apparently bought the picture with the express intention of presenting it to the National Gallery of his country of origin. Accordingly, it was despatched on the Anchor Line steamship *Furnessia*, which left New York on 23 April and arrived in Glasgow on 4 May 1887. Although well received in Edinburgh at the time (see *In Search of the Promised Land: Paintings by Frederic Edwin Church*, exhibition catalogue, Berry-Hill Galleries, Inc., New York, 2000, pp.57–8), the picture was subsequently overlooked and interest in Church on that side of the Atlantic waned, only to be rekindled nearly a century later by the spectacular sale in 1979 from a Manchester children's home of a hitherto lost painting, *Icebergs*, to the Museum of Fine Arts in Dallas.

The 1887 crossing was not the first time the painting travelled to Europe. It had originally been commissioned in 1866 by the New York dealer Michael Knoedler, who was also a selection committee member for the 1867 Paris *Exposition Universelle*. (See D. C. Huntington, *The Landscapes of F. E. Church: Vision of an American Era*, New York, 1966; *The Natural Paradise: Painting in America 1800–1850*, exhibition catalogue, Museum of Modern Art, New York, 1976; *Frederic Edwin Church*, exhibition catalogue, National Gallery of Art, Washington D.C., 1989–90, cat.no.40). For some reason Church did not, in the end, send the Edinburgh canvas to Paris as intended, and instead submitted his very well-known earlier horizontal version of this subject (now in the Corcoran Art Gallery, Washington), dating from 1857, which had been highly instrumental in establishing his reputation in the 1850s. The Edinburgh picture did travel to Europe soon after, however, and was exhibited in London for a month in 1868 at the McLean Gallery, Haymarket where it was well reviewed and even provoked favorable comparison with Turner. Its presence there also coincided with Church's first visit to Europe. Unlike many of his contemporaries he had, in the earlier part of his career, resisted the call of Europe and concentrated instead on depicting his native American scenery, very much influenced by his teacher Thomas Cole. His first trip abroad was, in fact, to South America in 1853.

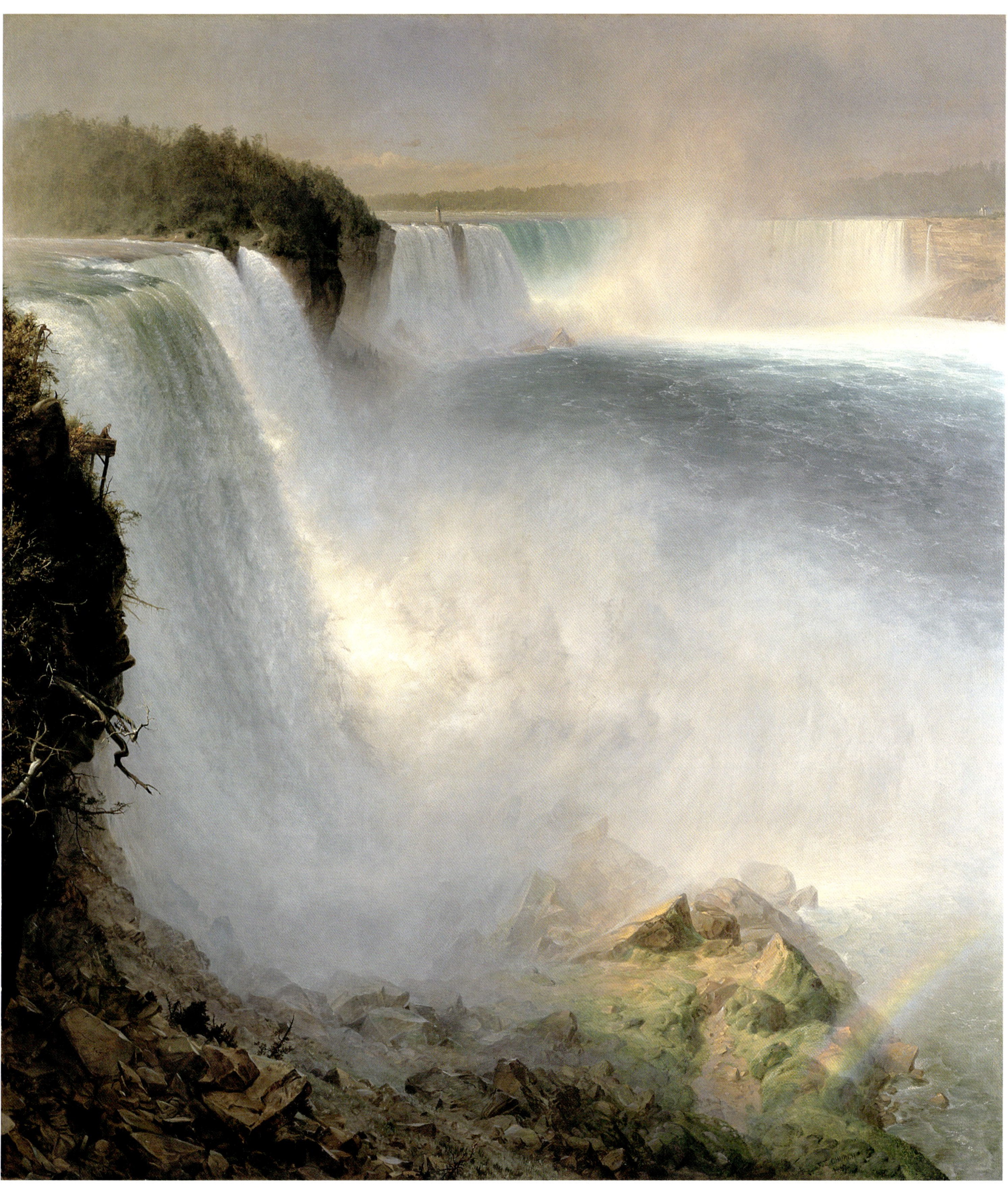

Index of Artists

The references given are to catalogue numbers